HAUNTED YBOR CITY

DEBORAH FRETHEM

Haunted America

Published by Haunted America
A Division of The History Press
Charleston, SC 29403
www.historypress.net

First published 2014

Manufactured in the United States

ISBN 978.1.62619.622.3

Library of Congress CIP data applied for.

Dedicated to all the people who told me I couldn't do it. And to all the people who believed I could. Most especially to Craig, who never waivers and who knows when to cajole and when to be stern. And to Signe, who calls me Bubba and kept asking, "When will your book be finished?"

CONTENTS

ACKNOWLEDGEMENTS

As always there are many people to thank. For research assistance, I need to thank the Tampa Historical Society Research Library, especially David for his help with historic photographs. Elizabeth McCoy at the Ybor City State Museum was also invaluable. And thanks are due to the University of South Florida Special Collections Library. I also want to thank the staff of the Ybor City Visitor Information Center, who proudly told me they were born in the *El Bien Público*. I am grateful to the many clerks, servers and other employees of shops and restaurants who were willing to share their stories with me. I am grateful to Scot Dietz, author of *Cigar City Mafia*, who showed my husband and me around the organized crime sites of Ybor and shared his insights and stories. Thanks go to Joe and Ybor City Historic Walking Tours; to Paul Guzzo, who first introduced me to the fascinating world of Charlie Wall; and as always, to the friends and family who supported me.

Introduction

THE BEGINNING OF A DREAM

Tampa was in trouble.

The little Florida settlement that had shown such promise in the first half of the nineteenth century was not doing well at the end of the Civil War. Malaria and yellow fever, hurricanes and war had all taken their toll. By 1885, the population had dropped from over one thousand to less than four hundred people. Some settlers had departed during the Civil War and never returned. Others had succumbed to the yellow fever epidemics that ravaged the area several times after 1850. The U.S. Army post, Fort Brooke, had been decommissioned in 1883. Even getting to Tampa was a challenge. It was either a long, uncomfortable stagecoach ride from Gainesville or an unreliable boat service over rough seas from Key West or Cedar Key. There was a strong possibility that Tampa would never recover. One historian called the 1870s the "dismal decade."

But two things happened to change all that. The first was the coming of a railroad, brought to Tampa by Henry B. Plant. Born in Connecticut in 1809, Henry grew up in the steamship era. As a young man, his grandmother offered to pay for him to be educated at Yale, but he turned down her offer. He wanted to learn the shipping business from the waterline up. He signed on as a deckhand on a steamship and worked his way to the top. He became an expert at moving cargo accurately and efficiently from place to place and quickly came to understand the value of rail transportation, expanding his business accordingly.

Elevated view of Tamp Box Company. This is where the cigar boxes were made. The building still stands and is being turned into apartments today. *Courtesy Tampa-Hillsborough Public Library System.*

Henry married in 1842 and had two sons, but his wife, Ellen Elizabeth, was often ill. A doctor suggested that she might do better in a warmer climate, so they spent some time in Jacksonville, Florida. The weather did seem to have recuperative powers for Ellen, but upon their return to the North, she once again fell ill, dying in 1861.

Distraught, Henry threw himself into his work. Despite his Connecticut background, he formed the Southern Express Company, which provided rail service to the Confederacy during the Civil War. His trains carried not only packages but also messages and money. And perhaps most importantly, they shipped home the bodies of the Confederate dead from the far-off battlefields. Many a Southern mother could actually bury her son in the family graveyard because of Henry B. Plant.

After the war, Henry used his connections to acquire the damaged and nearly destroyed railroads throughout the South, merging them into a new transportation system that made him a wealthy man. In 1883, phosphate, a mineral used to make fertilizer, was discovered in large amounts just southeast of Tampa. Henry Plant knew a moneymaking opportunity when he saw one, and he expanded his operation to include Tampa in 1884. But his rails did more than carry phosphate out of Florida. He also built two small hotels (both of which are long gone) and began to promote Tampa as a tourist destination. That way, his trains could carry passengers as well as freight. A few years later, in 1891, he would build the magnificent Tampa Bay Hotel, which is part of the University of Tampa today. Its silver domes and minarets are the symbol of Tampa.

But even a railroad was clearly not enough. The Bank of Tampa, the only such financial institution in the area, was packing up and getting ready to leave.

The second serendipitous occurrence that saved Tampa was the arrival of the cigar-making industry. And this almost didn't happen.

There were already cigar factories in the United States in New York and Key West. But the locations were not ideal, and several factory owners were looking for new sites. It was in 1884 that Gavino Gutiérrez, a Spaniard by birth, accompanied his friend, Bernardino Gárgol, a Cuban who ran an import business in New York City, to the Tampa Bay area in search of native guava trees in the hopes of increasing the manufacture of his most successful item, jellies and preserves made from the tropical fruit. Unfortunately, their search proved fruitless (no pun intended), and no guava trees were found. But Gutiérrez, who was familiar with several cigar makers, was very impressed with Tampa as a future cigar manufacturing area. The climate was ideal. Believe it or not, the humidity was a good thing for tobacco. Plant's new railroad allowed for easy shipping. And most important, the proximity to the tobacco fields of Cuba made importation of fine tobacco simple.

Gutiérrez contacted some other friends—Ignacio Haya and Vicente Martínez de Ybor—and encouraged them to come and look at this perfect location.

Ybor arrived in 1885 and found what he considered to be an ideal spot, forty acres northeast of Tampa. The land was owned by Captain John T. Leslie, a local pioneer and Civil War hero. Leslie wanted $9,000 to sell the property; Ybor only wanted to pay $5,000. Normally, this would have provided an opportunity for negotiations, but in this case, both men held firm, neither one budging on his price by so much as a dollar. Things were looking bleak, and Ybor prepared to leave Tampa to go to Galveston. (The Texas city was also courting Ybor and the others to establish their business there.)

Always the savvy investor, Ybor made sure that word of the impasse got to the Tampa Board of Trade, and it went into panic mode. The board begged Mr. Ybor to stay in town for a few more days and hastily called a meeting to deal with the problem. Finally, on October 5, 1885, Ybor agreed to meet Captain Leslie's price. And the board agreed to reimburse him the difference of $4,000. Ybor purchased the land immediately and began making plans for a "company town" that would employ, house and support hundreds of cigar workers. Workers began clearing the land on the very day the compromise was reached. The new town was christened Ybor City.

As time went on, more acreage was added to the original purchase, and other factory owners began to move their operations from Key West and New York to the new town on Tampa Bay.

Ironically, the honor of producing the very first Ybor City cigar did not go to Mr. Ybor and his *Príncipe de Gales* (Prince of Wales) factory. The original plan was for Ybor's factory and the factory of Ignacio Haya to open on the

Wood-frame Sánchez y Haya Factory Number One. The first Ybor City Cigar was made here. *Courtesy Tampa-Hillsborough Public Library System.*

same day. However, Mr. Ybor hired a Spanish foreman, and the Cuban cigar makers refused to work for a Spaniard. Further, the tobacco Mr. Haya used came from his factory in New York and had already been "stripped" (that is, the stems and nonusable parts removed), so it was one of his workers, Ramón Fernández, who produced the very first Ybor City cigar on Tuesday, April 1, 1886. Mr. Ybor's Spanish foreman was fired, and his factory also began producing fine cigars.

So successful were they that the City of Tampa annexed Ybor City on June 2, 1887, less than two years after it had been established. By the turn of the century, Ybor City's workers were hand rolling eight million cigars per week in more than two hundred factories. They were responsible for one-third of the annual income for the entire state of Florida.

There is a small irony about the name. Actually, in Spain and Cuba, the name is spelled *Ibor* and pronounced "ee-bore." The family changed the spelling when they first came to Key West, mainly because they were concerned that English speakers would mispronounce the original as "eye-bore." Its spelling doesn't seem to matter, for the name is frequently said wrong, even to this day.

And from its very beginnings, Ybor City had more than its share of the unusual and the macabre. Some spirits seem to have attached themselves to the land itself, even before the cigar factories began. And many believe that ghosts still walk the streets of Ybor City and linger in its old buildings. There are indeed spirits in cigar smoke.

Chapter 1

THE MAN AND HIS VISION

Certainly, the first ghost we should discuss would be the ghost of the founder himself. He was a complex man who believed in hard work and good luck. And he also believed that the harder you worked, the more good luck you would have.

Vicente Martínez de Ybor was born in Valencia, Spain, on September 7, 1818. His family had both wealth and position, but Vicente wanted to make his own way, although some believe that he was just trying to avoid the military service that was mandatory for all young Spanish men. He immigrated to Cuba at the age of fourteen and sought a job in the cigar industry, which was then in its infancy. He began as a lowly clerk and then became a broker. He opened his own factory in Havana in 1856. He was not yet forty years old.

His brand was *El Príncipe de Gales*, or "the Prince of Wales." The choice of title was not arbitrary. He wanted to convey a sense of connection with influence, power and wealth. The name also looks toward the future, as the Prince of Wales is the heir to the English throne; Ybor wanted to establish himself as the heir to the royalty of the cigar business. Furthermore, at the time he selected the name for his brand, the reigning Prince of Wales was Edward, son of Queen Victoria. The queen notoriously disapproved of smoking and forbade it at the British court. Edward (who would become King Edward VII in 1901) had a reputation for enjoying a fine cigar. Ybor hoped that smoking would be restored to respectability upon Edward's ascension to the British throne.

Today, it is easy to underestimate the importance of cigars to the gentlemen of the late nineteenth and early twentieth century. The men of the elite classes on both sides of the Atlantic would gather after dinner, without the presence of the ladies, to enjoy their brandy and cigars. It was considered sophisticated and even beneficial to one's health to smoke—not to mention masculine. Smoking was strictly for men. Pipe smoking had declined in popularity, and cigarettes, although available, were not yet in widespread use. What the wealthy did, the middle class would follow. And what the middle class did, the poor would follow. Most of the men in Europe and America smoked cigars. Ybor understood this and named his brand accordingly. It wasn't long before the factory in Havana was producing twenty thousand cigars a day.

Vicente Martínez de Ybor at about age sixty-eight. *Courtesy of the Ybor City State Museum.*

In 1848, Ybor married Palmia Learas, and they had four children before her death. He remarried in 1862. He and his second wife, Mercedes de las Revillas, would have eight more children, for a total of twelve in all.

Ybor was passionate about one thing other than his family and cigars. He was passionate about the cause of *Cuba Libre*, or a free Cuba. Despite his Spanish birth, he believed that colonial rule of Cuba by Spain was wrong. It is most likely true that his passion was not entirely altruistic. He resented the high taxes and tariffs placed on his products by the Spanish authorities. But for whatever reason, he became quite outspoken about his belief that Cuba should be independent. And he backed up his words by providing funds to Cuban rebels in the Ten Years' War for independence that broke out in 1868. Spanish authorities made plans to arrest him. So in 1869, he quietly slipped out of Cuba in disguise, taking his growing family and his growing business with him to Key West in Florida. Many of the rebels followed him and became workers in the factory he built there.

At first, the new location at the southernmost island in the United States was good to Ybor. He became the second-largest manufacturer of cigars in Key West. Indeed, he accumulated so much capital that he could loan funds to other manufacturers. He took pride that he had reinvested his profits into Key West.

But the limited land (the entire island of Key West is less than seven and a half square miles) and limited labor force made expansion difficult. And labor unrest began to be felt. There was a strong pro-union and pro-Marxist sentiment. The same attitudes that had brought the cigar workers from Cuba to Florida were flourishing in Key West. Ybor began to consider moving to another location. His first expansion was in New York City, where he built an enormous factory that he named El Coloso (the Colossus). And it was huge indeed. He employed five hundred workers in its five stories. But labor problems continued to plague him. And Northern unionists were better organized than those in Key West. El Coloso was beset by strikes in 1876 and 1877. He also found the climate in New York not only unpleasant but ill suited for tobacco as well, as it was far too dry. So he returned to the warmer temperatures and high humidity in Key West. But the last straw fell on the camel's back in 1886, when a great fire swept through Key West. Eleven of the major cigar factories were destroyed, along with about forty other buildings. Príncipe de Gales went up in the flames. So Ybor turned his eyes toward Tampa. He was sixty-eight years old when he founded the city that bears his name. Despite his age, he became the proud papá of Ybor City.

His first factory, a wood-frame structure, was soon replaced by a large brick building that stands to this day. When it was completed, it was the largest cigar factory in the world and filled a city block.

Ybor tried to be a fair man. He wanted to avoid the labor unrest that he had suffered in Key West and New York, and to that end, he paid generous wages and tried to give his workers good living conditions. He built small houses, known as *casitas*, which his workers could purchase at cost and with easy payment terms. He believed that home ownership would give stability to his workforce. He also became involved in several other businesses that would provide a complete community, including a brewery, a hotel, a gas company, an ice factory and a brick factory. Although the roads were just mud at first, they were soon replaced with cobblestone streets and wooden sidewalks and high curbs, which kept the alligators off. By 1890, his Príncipe de Gales was producing 900,000 hand-rolled cigars per month.

He built his own home to be near his factory and workers, although it was far more palatial than the *casitas*. He called it La Quinta, or the Country House.

After several successful years, Vicente passed away on December 14, 1896. His contribution to the city was recognized, as nearly the entire city shut

View of *casitas*, or workers' row houses, along a dirt road. *Courtesy Tampa-Hillsborough Public Library System.*

down for the funeral. All the dignitaries of the area, including the railroad baron Henry B. Plant, the mayor and city council, were in attendance. The headline in the *Tampa Tribune* read, "Great Benefactor Gone." At the time of his death, he owned so many businesses and so much real estate that his partners concluded there was not enough capital in Tampa to liquidate his assets; it actually took almost ten years to settle his vast estate.

He was interred in the Tampa City Cemetery, in the St. Louis Roman Catholic section. But he was not buried. At the end of his life, Mr. Ybor had made it clear to his heirs that, although he loved Tampa and Ybor City, his heart remained in Cuba, even after all these years. His last request was that his body be sent to Cuba as its final resting place. However, since the Spanish-American War was looming on the horizon at the time, it was deemed necessary to place his body "temporarily" in an impressive vault above ground. The plan was for his body to be moved to Cuba when the war was over and his family could move it to its final resting place.

It has been 118 years now (as of 2014), and still his body is here. And as of today, there are no plans to ever move it. But there are some who say that Vicente Martínez de Ybor does not rest in peace. The figure of a balding, mustached man wearing a dark suit, black bow tie and round spectacles has been seen wandering the grounds at night. Those who have seen him say he has a lost and puzzled look. Perhaps he is simply wondering, "What part of Cuba is this?"

And the old cemetery (now known as Oaklawn) might not be the only place his spirit still walks. He has been seen in the courtyard of his brick factory complex, which still stands. His hazy image seems lost in thought, as he contemplates the structures around him, almost as if he is planning the next expansion of his business. And of course, he is smoking a cigar. The lit end glows with a red-orange light, and the smell of fine Cuban tobacco fills the air.

Chapter 2

SPIRITS IN THE FACTORIES

The cigar factories of Ybor City made only one kind of cigar, "Clear Havana." That is defined as a cigar made in the United States but from exclusively Cuban tobacco. It must also be made entirely by hand and in exactly the same style and manner of workmanship as those employed in Cuban factories. And the factories of Ybor City were extremely successful, producing millions of cigars each year.

Although these facilities were called factories, they were nothing like the factories in the northeast United States at that time. Although the tobacco did go through a processing system, there really was no assembly line. Once tobacco reached the table of the actual cigar rollers, the *torcedores*, the process was completed by one skilled individual, more or less at his own pace. These workers were well paid, though their pay was based on the number of cigars they produced. They were respected as artisans of their craft. There was so much pride in the product that it is not a surprise that some of their spirits linger in the old buildings even though cigars are no longer made there.

There were other types of factories in Ybor City as well, including a brewery founded by Mr. Ybor himself. That beautiful building stands to this day.

Cigar workers in the gallery. *Courtesy Tampa-Hillsborough Public Library System.*

YBOR SQUARE

One of the first things Ybor did after purchasing his land was to hire a local builder, C.E. Purcell, to construct a three-story wooden factory and housing for fifty workers. The first challenge was the terrain itself. Much of Ybor's new land was a marsh, teeming with alligators and panthers and infested by mosquitoes. Literally thousands of loads of sand were brought in and dumped on the swamp in order to make it buildable.

Mr. Ybor believed that he could ensure the loyalty of his workers by giving them a vested interest in the success of the business and the town. He wanted them to feel like they were part of a community. To that end, he developed Ybor City as a "company town" that could provide for all the workers' needs, from housing to social clubs. So he built not just a factory but also homes and facilities for the cigar makers.

That first wooden factory was always meant to be temporary, and while it was still under construction, work began on its replacement. The final result was to be a far larger, four-story, brick structure. This is the building that still stands today on the corner of Eighth Avenue and Avenue República de Cuba (Fourteenth Street). Made out of red brick, with wrought-iron steps and fencing, the structure has windows, trimmed in white, that face north and south to maximize the light and ventilation for the workers. There is a glass cupola on top of the building. The cupola was originally open air but was later enclosed. It served as a lookout station. An employee would be dispatched to that cupola every day to keep an eye on the harbor. If he saw a ship arriving from Havana, he would let the factory managers know so that a railroad car could be sent to meet the boat to bring the fresh supplies back for processing.

After Vicente Ybor's death in 1895, the factory was run by his business partner, Edward Manrara, but only for a few years. In 1899, the complex was sold to the Havana America Company. Two years after that, it became the property of the American Cigar Company. In 1954, it was purchased by the Hava-A-Tampa company, which used it only for storage and for shipping operations. It ceased to be a factory. In 1972, the buildings were sold again to Trend Publications. It wanted to build a shopping mall in Ybor and intended to use the complex as headquarters. The company preserved the historic exterior, although it did take down the water tower. The huge interior workrooms were also maintained. Over the next few years, several different enterprises called this place home. And although it is no longer a factory, Ybor's brick masterpiece is still a very busy place.

The full city block where the factory building stands now encompasses a restaurant called the Spaghetti Warehouse and the offices of a free local newspaper, *Creative Loafing*, which specializes in arts and entertainment throughout the Tampa Bay Area. The rest of the huge complex was purchased by the Church of Scientology and is now the headquarters of that organization in Tampa. But all this activity does not seem to have discouraged the spirits of the past.

Ybor City Ghost Walk is an audio tour that can be downloaded and followed at your leisure. It tells a fascinating tale of a young woman named Rosalita. Living in Cuba, she found herself pregnant and unmarried. Her family sent her to Ybor City to avoid the shame of her child's illegitimacy. She gave birth in Florida, and the baby was adopted by a fine Cuban family. However, having no money to return to Cuba, Rosalita needed to find a way to support herself. Unable to find a job as a *tabaquero* (tobacco worker), she turned to prostitution. Despite the difficulties of this life, she did manage to find love, with a sailor who had come to visit Ybor City.

When he sailed away, he promised Rosalita that he would return. But days, weeks and then months went by. Rosalita's sailor never returned to her. Still, every evening, she would climb to the little glass room at the top of Señor Ybor's factory and look out over the harbor in the hopes of seeing his ship. No one knows exactly when Rosalita died, but since her death, if you look up into the cupola just at dusk, you will see the figure of a dark-haired woman gazing out of the windows. This story may very well be apocryphal, but there have been several people who claim to have seen a shadowy figure in the cupola when no one should be there. Is it the ghost of Rosalita? Or perhaps the ghost of one of the young employees whose job it was to keep watch over the harbor?

Those who sit for a few moments in the courtyard of the old factory also say they hear the sound of muted voices, speaking Spanish, as if several people were holding casual conversations. When they look in the direction of the sounds, there is no one there. On other occasions, people have reported the sound of a deep, resonant baritone voice, speaking rather loudly, also in what sounds like Spanish. The voice does not seem conversational but rather as if the owner of that voice is giving a performance or a lecture. Those who describe this situation are uncertain how such a voice would fit in with the history of the factory. But there is a very real connection.

El lector, or "the reader," was one of the most important people in a cigar factory, even though he never laid hands on tobacco leaves. He was hired by the workers themselves to read to them during the long workday. He would read for two hours in the morning, usually the local newspapers, and two hours in the afternoon, often a novel chosen by a committee of workers. The qualifications for the job were quite rigorous. The *lector* had to have a fine, booming speaking voice in order to be heard over the sounds of the gallery, where the cigar makers sat at their tables. And of course, there was no microphone or other amplification. He had to speak beautiful, pure Castilian Spanish. And he had to be able to translate from English-language newspapers and novels "on the fly" and without hesitation. When he read from novels, the workers expected a performance similar to what we would call a "radio play" today, with different voices for the characters and a dramatic reading of the narrative. If the performance were good, the workers would show their approval by tapping their *chavetas* (round cutting knives used in the cigar rolling process). If the performance were not what they had hoped for, the workers could be ruthless with catcalls and other verbal signs of their displeasure. Each worker contributed to the reader's pay, and he made about seventy-five dollars a week during an era when the average cigar maker earned twenty dollars a week. It is not a surprise that the spirit of such an important person would linger at the old factory.

Although Afro-Cubans worked side by side with other Cubans and other nationalities in the factories, there was only one Afro-Cuban who achieved the coveted role of reader. His name was Faccundo Accione. There was also one female reader. Her name was Luisa Capetillo. She dressed just like a man, in a suit and tie, and wore a fedora hat. She described herself as a "socialist anarchist." She wanted all wealth and property to be shared, but she wanted it done without any form of government. "Brotherhood as the supreme law, without frontiers or divisions of race, color, or language," she said. She worked only briefly in Ybor City—most likely her extreme views were as much a negative as her gender at the time.

Another famous *lector* was Victoriano Monteiga. He arrived in Ybor City from Cuba in 1913 at the age of only nineteen with ten dollars in his pockets. But his beautiful voice, which was said to sometimes make women weep, soon got him a job as a reader. Often the women of the area would gather outside the factory windows so that they could hear him read.

In the early years, the owners of the factories welcomed the readers. They felt it kept the workers from chatting too much with one another, which increased production and kept the workers from banding together to form a union. But as time went on, the owners began to view the readers as the very center of labor unrest. They felt the newspaper articles, and even the novels being read, were too radical in nature, perhaps even Communist. Even though it was the workers themselves who chose what was read, the owners blamed the readers and tried to have them banned. This actually led to the very thing the owners feared: strikes by the workers. Several times the workers won the right to keep the *lectores*, but after the strike of 1932, all the readers were gone.

Victoriano Monteiga found himself out of a job. He had always preferred working with his brains rather than with his hands, and in 1922, he had started his own newspaper. *La Gaceta* is still published to this day. It is trilingual, featuring articles in English, Spanish and Italian. Victoriano passed the publishing of the paper to his son, Roland, in 1961. Roland was famous for his political column "As We Heard It." He developed such an uncanny ability to predict the results of elections that his opinion and endorsement was sought by many significant candidates including Jimmy Carter and George H.W. Bush. Roland passed away in 1998. At the time of Roland's death, his son Patrick, who was already working for the newspaper as an associate editor, became editor in chief. He also continued the "As We

Arango y Arango Inc. Cigar Factory. *Courtesy Tampa-Hillsborough Public Library System.*

Heard It" column. Three generations have brought *La Gaceta* to the people of Ybor City. And it all began from the position of reader.

Strange things have happened in the Spaghetti Warehouse that occupies part of the tobacco warehouse section of the complex. Customers and servers have reported the sound of footsteps when there is no one there and cold spots materializing for no apparent reason. Paranormal investigators believe that when a spirit is trying to manifest itself, it will gather all the heat and energy from the air as it strives to make an appearance, leaving a cold spot behind. Who might be struggling to make his or her presence known in Ybor's old factory complex? For the past few years, a troupe of actors called MurderS She Wrote has been doing a monthly participatory murder-mystery play in the Spaghetti Warehouse. Perhaps the old spirits are being made restless by the fact that an imaginary murder takes place there on a monthly basis.

OLIVA TOBACCO WAREHOUSE

A lot of Ybor City's original buildings still stand, although many have been repurposed. The three-story building on Palm Avenue and North Eighteenth Street was built in 1900 as a wood-frame structure, but after the great fire of 1908, it was remodeled with a fire-resistant exterior. It originally housed the Monett Cigar Factory. In 1980, it became the warehouse and offices for the Oliva Tobacco Company and remained in its hands until 1999. After that, like many other former factories, it sat empty gathering debris, dust, pigeons and rats.

In 2007, two brothers, Blake and James Emory, rented the decrepit old building. They enlisted a large group of volunteers, who helped them clear out the debris, clean and apply fresh coats of paint to the walls. Being artists themselves, they hoped to establish a haven for artists of all kinds. They produced plays and displayed sculpture and paintings. Then they got some bad news. The owner had decided to sell the property to a developer who wanted to put up a hotel on the site.

The brothers were sorry to lose their artist's space, but they knew they were also leaving something else behind—the ghostly spirits that seemed to be haunting the building. Several encounters had convinced them that phantoms of the past roamed about. On one occasion, near an upstairs window, Blake saw the apparition of a man wearing a hat walking briskly away from him and then vanishing. Fleeting shadowy figures have been seen in one room on the second floor. When the Emory brothers spent the night, sleeping on the floor, they awoke to voices muttering in a foreign language. Perhaps most intriguing of all, a visitor once decided to investigate an old bathroom on the ground floor. The room was windowless, and the plumbing was no longer functional. So it was curiosity that led the young man into the room. He shut the door behind him. When he tried to leave, the door would not open. He said it seemed as if someone were holding the door closed from the outside. He assumed that this was being done by a human being, not a ghost. But when he was finally able to get the door opened, there was no one around.

Once they did try to conduct a séance on the second level. As they extinguished the lights and sat down on the dusty, wooden floor, they heard the sound of shattering glass. Quickly, they snapped the lights back on, and the floor was actually covered with fine shards of glass. However, there was no source for the glass in the room. Where did it come from?

Blake and James wanted to learn more about the spirits they had encountered, so they invited the Florida Ghost Team, paranormal investigators, to explore the old factory. On the second floor, the group got an immediate response to their question "Is anybody here with us?" They heard a loud bang, followed by the sound of something quite heavy being dragged across the floor. When they focused their flashlights in the direction of the sound, there was nothing there. As the team continued to explore on the second level, they heard the sound of footsteps above them on the third floor. When they went up to investigate, there was no one there. The inside of the building was stifling and hot, so they decided to go outside for a breath of fresh air. They distinctly heard the sound of footsteps, as if someone were running up behind them. When they whirled around, again, there was no one to be seen. Perhaps the most interesting result from their investigation came when they were listening to what they had recorded while in the old factory. On the recorder, when they asked, "Is anyone here with us?" there came a whispered, but definite, answer in a woman's voice, "Me."

Who are these spirits? We have no certain answers. It is unlikely they are from the time of the Oliva Tobacco Company, as that was quite recent, from 1980 to 1999. Also, during that time, it was a warehouse, not a factory. The Oliva Tobacco Company does not make cigars. It supplies tobacco to the makers of fine cigars, and it is still in business, now in West Tampa.

It is most likely that they are the spirits of those who worked in the factory years ago. It is unlikely that we will ever know their names.

THE FLORIDA BREWING COMPANY

Before there was Tampa, there was Fort Brooke. Before that, there were the Seminoles. Before that, there were the Spanish, and before that, there were the native peoples—the Timucua, the Tocobaga and the Caloosa. In fact, it was the Caloosa who gave Tampa its name. Theirs was a large tribe that extended from the southern shores of Tampa Bay nearly to what is now Miami. They called the great bay *tampa*, which in their language meant "sticks of fire." Most likely this was a reference to the many lightning strikes that hit the area in the summer months.

Long before the arrival of the Spanish conquistadors in the sixteenth century, the various tribes would gather at a sacred spring near Tampa Bay. Because it was a place of peace and healing, tribal differences and quarrels

Factory of the Florida Brewing Company at Fifth Avenue and Thirteenth Street. *Courtesy Tampa-Hillsborough Public Library System.*

were put aside. But when the Spaniards arrived on these shores, they brought with them diseases that decimated the ancient tribes, and the sacred spring was forgotten.

The land lay empty and quiet for years until the Seminoles began to settle in Florida. The word *seminole* is actually a corruption of a Spanish word *cimarrón*, which means "runaway" or "wild one." Originally these people were part of the Creek nations in northern Florida, Georgia and Alabama, but in the eighteenth century, they separated themselves from the Creek culture. They intermarried with free blacks, many of whom were formerly enslaved persons who had escaped their bondage. This new band moved farther south into central Florida. But as often happened in the early days of the United States, pioneers and settlers began to covet land held by Native Americans. Invariably this led to conflict. In 1824, Florida was a territory, acquired by the United States from Spain just a few years before. Wanting to secure the new territory, the U.S. government sent Colonel George Mercer Brook to establish a fort where the Hillsborough River flows into Tampa Bay. The stated purpose of this fort was to control the Seminole population and "protect" the white settlers. Named Fort Brooke, after its commander, it was a small wooden fort. Just a few soldiers, probably bored and lonely, manned its walls. But these soldiers rediscovered the ancient spring. They immediately claimed its pure waters for their own use. It became known as the "Government Spring."

At the end of the three "Seminole Wars," most of the Native Americans were transported along the "Trail of Tears" to Indian Territory, west of the Mississippi River. Fewer than two hundred Seminoles remained in Florida, fleeing to the Everglades and doing their best to preserve their culture.

But Fort Brooke remained, and it soon became important in the U.S. Civil War. The small skirmish called the Battle of Fort Brooke was actually fought nearby in 1863. On May 6, 1864, the fort and the town of Tampa surrendered to Union forces. After the war, the fort declined along with the rest of Tampa. Decommissioning followed in 1883. The Government Spring remained.

It was just a few years later that those waters became important once again. Vicente Martínez de Ybor was involved in many businesses other than cigars, and he soon saw the need for a brewery. He wanted to provide liquid refreshment for his workers to purchase, but he also wanted to export beer to Cuba. And what is one of the most important ingredients in good beer? Water, of course. The water from the old Government Spring was there on the edge of Ybor City. So Ybor formed a partnership with a Cuban-born friend named Edward Manrara. Although considerably younger, Manrara made the perfect business partner for Ybor. He was well educated and bilingual. His ability to read and write in both English and Spanish was an invaluable asset. Don Vicente himself had a very limited command of English.

Together the two men formed the Florida Brewing Company in 1896. The beautiful building, which still stands at 1220 to 1235 Fifth Avenue, cost $200,000 to build and was modeled after the Castle Brewery in Johannesburg. The appearance is therefore more Dutch than Spanish, which is somewhat unexpected in Ybor City. Its impressive height of seventy-five feet (six stories) made it the tallest building in Tampa at the time, and although its height has been surpassed by the downtown skyscrapers, it remains the tallest building in Ybor City as of this writing.

A grand opening celebration was held on February 15, 1897. It was to be a huge party. The invitation was actually published in the local newspaper and included nearly everyone. "White or black, rich or poor" were all encouraged to attend. A "day of merry making" was promised with music, speeches, food and, of course, beer—lots and lots of beer. The party included twenty carcasses of barbecued beef and barrels of pickles. But the main attraction was four hundred barrels of lager beer. Decorations included two large stuffed alligators sitting upright on the food table. Each had a bottle of beer stuck in its mouth. On another table there was a life-sized wooden carving of a Seminole Indian chief, crowned with Spanish moss and holding the company logo in his hands.

Ybor and Manrara had hired an excellent brew master named Anton Birhbaum, who insisted that his beer was so pure that it was not intoxicating, even though it was hardy and certainly had the normal alcohol content. It did not take long for Mr. Birhbaum to be proved wrong. As the party raged on, two men reached for the same glass of beer. One was a Cuban cigar worker named Eduardo Sandoval. The other was an Irishman who worked in the icehouse, Dan Hogan. The two men exchanged heated words, there was some cursing in both English and Spanish and the final result was Hogan slamming a beer stein down on Sandoval's head. Unfortunately, the Cuban man died from the blow, and some believe that his spirit has never left the scene of the party and his demise. Apparently, the death did nothing to dampen the high spirits of the rest of those in attendance.

On February 15, 1898, exactly one year later, the U.S. battleship the *Maine*, which had been sent to Havana Harbor to protect American interests in Cuba, mysteriously exploded. This precipitated the Spanish-American War. American generals planned that war in Tampa, sitting on the front porch of Henry Plant's Tampa Bay Hotel along the shores of the Hillsborough River. One of the officers was a young Theodore Roosevelt. He and his "Rough Riders" rode their horses through the Florida Brewery one afternoon, helping themselves to liquid refreshment. Now that is certainly "rough" riding!

Despite these minor setbacks at the start, the Florida Brewing Company went on to become very successful. During the Labor Day parade in 1900, the tradition of giving away free beer continued. The Florida Brewing Company entered a float that looked like a huge beer barrel, and indeed, it was filled with actual lager beer. All along the parade route, Tampans were able to slake their thirst from that enormous barrel. Legend has it that by the time the parade was over, there wasn't enough beer left in that barrel to intoxicate a mosquito.

Although hit by fire in both 1906 and 1909, the brewery always managed to bounce back. It added a distilling system for liquor and expanded its bottling capabilities. By 1913, the brewery was producing two hundred

The Florida Brewery Building today. *Author's collection.*

barrels of beer per day. Even Prohibition didn't slow it down, and the brewery continued to operate, brewing beer for local consumption as well as for export to Cuba. Finally, it was raided by federal agents in 1927. Salvador Martínez Ybor, the son of the founder, was brought to trial, fined $100 and sentenced to six months in jail. However, that sentence was reversed on appeal. Nevertheless, the Florida Brewing Company had to temporarily shut down. At the end of Prohibition, it reorganized as the Tampa, Florida Brewing Company and resumed doing business.

But times finally caught up with the old brewery. In 1961, an embargo was placed on Cuba due to the rise of the Castro regime. And even worse, a very large competitor arrived on the scene, Anheuser-Busch Company. Florida Brewing closed its doors in 1962. For a few years, the building was used as a storage place for fresh tobacco. Some of the original doors and windows were bricked over. Part of the building was designated as a "fallout shelter" during the cold war. Eventually, it just sat empty and began to decay.

Finally, in 1999, the crumbling building was purchased by **Dale Swope** and Joseph Kokolakis. By that time, it was so decrepit that many thought it was beyond saving. But the new owners were not to be deterred. **Dale Swope**, who wanted the building to house his law firm, was particularly enthusiastic. The restoration and renovation took over a year and cost $6 million. It was certainly a challenge. The old structure had become a maze of dark and twisting corridors. Floors did not all meet at the same level. Lightning had done considerable damage to the tower in the 1970s.

Dale told the *St. Petersburg Times* (now the *Tampa Bay Times*) he loves all the artifacts discovered during the rehabilitation. He is using old wooden beer cases as tables and a broken beer bottle as a pencil holder. When a jury renders a favorable verdict for one of his clients, Dale has a red-and-blue flag flown from the brewery tower. He also said that "it is a great happiness" to work in the historic building "because it's just so cool."

Dale Swope is also one of the people who reports hauntings in the old building. "We do have a ghost here at the brewery company," he told the *St. Petersburg Times* in October 2002. He said the presence was first noticed right after construction began. In parts of the building that had been closed up since at least the 1960s, people heard sounds of a "very drunk man" with a heavy Hispanic accent. They thought it was a homeless person hiding in the maze of hallways. But even though they searched for the man, they never found anyone. Even after construction ended, the continued to hear laughter and mutterings. Dale is apparently quite a brave man, for when he heard the sounds, he would grab a flashlight and set off, searching the fire escapes and stairwells. Again, no one was ever found. Dale says whoever the spirit may be, he doesn't bother anyone. He simply makes his presence known through the sound of his voice. Could this be the spirit of poor Eduardo Sandoval, who was struck down on the very day the brewery opened? Perhaps he is still angry that, even after his untimely demise, the celebration went on.

Some people have offered another possible explanation as to who the ghost might be. In 1968, the eminent Tampa historian Anthony Pizzo wrote about what he called "the first legal hanging in Tampa," which supposedly happened in 1850. But there is a persistent mystery surrounding the case.

What we do know for certain is that on December 4, 1849, behind Antonio Castello's oyster house in Tampa, a body was discovered. The victim was a Fort Brooke soldier named Thomas Cline. He had been shot in the back. There were no witnesses, and there was no immediate suspect. It wasn't long, however, before suspicion fell on a local man, who had come from Cuba. His name was José Perfino (some accounts give his name as José Epperfino), and he had a bad reputation. Most folks thought he was a pirate, and he had a nasty temper. He was arrested for the murder but was soon released for lack of evidence.

It wasn't long after that new evidence (records do not say what that evidence was) was miraculously discovered. José was arrested again and tried on Friday, April 12, 1850. The presiding judge was Joseph Lancaster, who would later become the first mayor of Tampa, and the jury was made up of the area's foremost citizens, including William Ashley, who would become the first city clerk of Tampa. José pleaded not guilty. The verdict did not take long as it was rendered that very afternoon: "We the jury, find the prisoner at the bar Guilty of Murder, and so say we all." Sentencing was put off until the next day, so it was on an unlucky thirteenth of the month that José was sentenced to be taken to the Government Spring (future site of the Florida Brewing Company), where he was to be hanged by the neck until he was "Dead! Dead! Dead!" According to Anthony Pizzo, the usual words of "And the Lord have mercy on his soul" were scratched out. Pizzo goes on to speculate that the reason for the vehemence of the condemnation was part of the anti–Native American sentiment of the day. José's nickname was *El Indio*, so he was probably of Native American ancestry and appearance, possibly a mixed-race Seminole. Pizzo also implies that the sentence was carried out as scheduled on Friday, May 17, 1850 (seventeen is considered an unlucky number in Latino cultures), but he admits that the records are "exasperatingly silent."

However, it appears from other records that the hanging never took place. According to official documents of the governor at the time, Thomas Brown (second governor of the state of Florida from October 1849 to October 1853), José Perfino escaped from jail six days before the scheduled execution. Governor Brown offered a $100 reward from the State of Florida to the person who would bring José to justice, dead or alive. Official records of the Florida state legislature confirm that José was hunted down by a posse from Fort Brooke and then shot "while trying to escape," and these records also confirm that one Private Michael Daly was granted the state's reward for presenting the body to authorities.

Perhaps this makes little difference. Whether he was guilty or innocent, hanged or shot, José Perfino was just as dead. He is buried in Oaklawn Cemetery. His gravestone reads:

Jose Perfino
Cuban Pirate
El Indio
Killed 1850

It is worth noting that the marker on his tomb says "killed" rather than "hanged"; there are other gravestones nearby of lynched or executed individuals, and their stones all specify "hanged." And it does not mean that the ghost of José is not responsible for the strange sounds of a man with a Hispanic accent in the brewery. Even if he died elsewhere, his spirit might return to the site where he was supposed to have died.

Some historians have gone so far as to suggest that it may have been the name on this tombstone that inspired Juan Gómez, another early Spanish settler, to invent the legend of a Spanish pirate named José Gaspar, a legend that continues to "haunt" Tampa to this day.

Chapter 3

BAD MEN

MURDERERS AND GANGSTERS

It is perhaps true that Ybor City has had more than its share of bizarre crimes and career criminals. These macabre stories are interesting in and of themselves, but most of them have a haunting associated with them as well.

FREDERICK WEIGHTNOVEL

One of the most notorious parties in the history of Tampa happened in Ybor City sometime around 1887. It was the scandalous "Free Love Society Banquet," and it took place at the Hotel de La Havana. It was an orgiastic feast that featured all manner of aphrodisiacs and nude mulatto waitresses. It was the grand idea of one of the Tampa Bay area's best-known eccentrics, Frederick Leontiff Weightnovel. Yes, Tampa has always attracted its share of colorful characters, but the good doctor was perhaps the most bizarre of all.

Dr. Frederick Weightnovel came to the Tampa area from Russia, probably around 1880. Was that his real name? Was he even a doctor? The answers are unknown. However, we do know that he applied for membership in the Hillsborough County Medical Association—and that his request was denied.

Weightnovel claimed to have been imprisoned by the czar for advocating a violent overthrow of the Russian monarchy. He said that he managed to escape Siberia by swimming across an icy river. A tall and heavyset fellow with a huge barrel chest, he let his hair and beard grow long. In fact, he claimed that he had vowed that if he ever escaped Siberia, he would never cut his hair and beard again. All this gave him an appearance that earned him the nickname of the "Mad Russian," a sort of Tampa version of Rasputin.

Moving into a building on Whiting Street between Franklin and Tampa Streets, he developed a thriving business in "patent medicines." Today we might call him a "snake oil salesman." He sold tonics that he claimed had highly beneficial effects for both men and women. Among other things, he claimed that his tonics would "restore manhood." (The nineteenth-century version of Viagra?) He also claimed he could cure baldness. Ever a man with a huge ego, he made sure his wild-haired likeness was on every bottle of every one of his "cures."

His marketing techniques were unorthodox, to say the least. He would head down to Tampa Bay on warm afternoons and simply float on his back for hours, eating his dinner (often a plate of oysters, renowned for their aphrodisiac qualities) from a silver tray balanced on his ponderous belly, reading the newspaper or smoking a cigar. When a crowd would gather to watch him, he would take the opportunity to promote his restorative products. He also was one of the first people to use a business card. He had cards made, showing his picture, complete with his long, wild gray hair and shaggy beard. The card was printed in both English and Spanish and claimed that he was a graduate of the Russian Imperial Moscow University from 1863.

Of course, in those days, that kind of claim would have been difficult to verify. But Weightnovel did have his fans. A wealthy woman named Julia Daniels Moseley, who spent a few months in Florida, hired him to be her personal physician, and she adored him. She said in a letter to her sister in the North, "He is very odd, very smart, and has wandered nearly all over the world. He is a scholar, something of a writer and a lover of nature."

But Weigtnovel had his detractors as well. And he had his share of legal difficulties. His first problems with the law came in 1883. The abandonment of Fort Brooke left the area open to homesteaders. Weightnovel recruited a group of followers, who attempted to found their own town on the abandoned property. It was intended to be a utopian, socialist community. Weightnovel went so far as to appoint himself the mayor of the new town, which they named Moscow. However, Tampa authorities were not amused by this upstart town within their own borders, and the local police broke up the commune, evicting the members from the property.

The second brush with the law was that wild party in Ybor City. This had some serious consequences, although it seems amusing by today's standards. Sometime in the mid-1880s, Dr. Weightnovel, ever the radical, decided that Tampa needed a "Free Love Society." He became the club's founder and president. He believed that the fullest expression of health was the physical union of a man and a woman. And he didn't think marriage should limit that coupling.

It was a fine evening when the members of the Tampa Free Love Society, including about thirty of the most eligible bachelors in the area, got together. They dressed in handsome pseudo-military attire and rode on horseback to the gathering in Ybor City. Most folks in Ybor were pretty tolerant, much more so than downtown Tampans. That is most likely the reason for the selection of the Hotel de La Havana as the site of the festivities. However, no one bothered to close the curtains. While they might have ignored it had it been kept private, the citizens did not like having to witness the orgy. Weightnovel and all his cronies were hauled off to jail. Although he was only there for a few days, he said that Tampa jails were horrible, worse than being imprisoned in Siberia. He vowed to never spend any time in jail again.

In 1903, Weightnovel was involved in another scrape with the law. As far as Tampa was concerned, it was the trial of the century. Of course, there were ninety-seven years to go.

It seems the "doctor" had begun to branch out in the services he offered. Besides patent medicines, he had begun to run a "health clinic" on the second floor of his building. One of the services he offered was to "help" women who found themselves with an unwanted pregnancy. Dr. Weightnovel began to perform abortions—and not just for the local women of the streets. He offered his services to the wealthy and elite of Tampa as well.

The trial concerned the death of a young woman by the name of Irene Randall. She had come to see him in 1902, seeking to end a pregnancy. Something must have gone terribly wrong, for after the procedure, she developed a raging infection. Believing that she was dying, Irene begged Dr. Weightnovel to send for her mother. She wanted to see her one last time. He promised he would send for the woman, but he never did. In her few lucid moments, Irene would go to the window of her room and gaze out at the street, hoping to see her mother, who, of course, never came.

After about a week, Weightnovel became concerned enough to summon a real physician to consult on the case. He called on Dr. B.G. Abernathy, an actual member of the Hillsborough County Medical Association, to come to examine Irene. Of course, he did not tell Abernathy the full truth about what had happened. He claimed that when Irene came to see him, she had already taken "strong medicine" that had caused a miscarriage. However, when Dr. Abernathy spoke to Irene, she told him the truth about what happened. She also told him how Weightnovel had promised to contact her mother, but she was sure that he had never done so. Abernathy was unable to do anything to help the girl, and she passed from this life to the next in his arms on the very afternoon he met her. Or did she?

Frederick Weightnovel was brought to trial for manslaughter. The testimony included a particularly brutal description of the operation performed on Irene. Dr. Abernathy was the star witness, describing the desperate state of the young woman by the time he had been called in. "She told me that she was dying and wanted to send a message to her mother," he said. "And that Dr. Weightnovel had promised her that he would telegraph her mother, but had not done so."

After a four-day trial, Weightnovel was found guilty. He appealed his case to the Florida Supreme Court but lost there as well. He was sentenced to serve a six-year term of hard labor in prison, which actually seems like a light sentence considering the severity of his crime. However, even one day in jail was more than he wanted to face. He poisoned himself—perhaps by drinking too much of his own patent medicines—so that he never served anytime.

Some believe that both his spirit and the spirit of Irene still haunt the corner of Franklin and Whiting. But it also appears that he haunts Ybor City.

The Hotel de La Havana was located on the corner of Seventh Avenue (also known as La Gran Séptima Avenida) and Nineteenth Street. According to the historic plaque that now stands there, it was a three-story frame structure and was the first hotel built in in Ybor. Its proprietors were José Rubia and Jacinto Olavarria. Unfortunately, the building was destroyed during the first great fire in March 1891. Although the hotel itself no longer stands, the memory of Dr. Weightnovel's infamous evening of debauchery still lingers. There are still reports of the sound of hoofbeats moving down La Séptima approaching the site of the old hotel even though there are no horses in the area, and the sounds of revelry and loud drunken voices seem to come out of nowhere. One of those drunken voices seems louder than the others and has a distinct Russian accent, which is definitely unusual in an area where mainly Spanish and Italian are heard. Perhaps Frederick Weightnovel just wants to keep the party going,

ROBERT ANDERSON

Ybor City has been known for many things over the years—cigars, fine Cuban food, raucous parades and exotic nightlife. What one doesn't think of in connection with Ybor City is serial killers. And yet one of the very first serial killers in the United States did his horrible deeds right on those very streets.

Terror began to stalk the good citizens of Ybor City late in 1911, and it lasted for seven horrendous months. On Christmas Eve, the night watchman of Tampa Steam Ways, a shipping company, was found dead, clearly murdered. Then just after the New Year, an African American man was found murdered. He was never identified. Other murders followed on May 29 and June 30. The latter victim was Edward Geary, who was also a night watchman for the Tampa Steam Ways company. There was no suspect. In fact, police weren't even sure these murders were connected.

On April 9, 1912, an anonymous letter was thrown over the wall and into the yard of the Hillsborough County jail. The letter writer stated that he was an African American man and that he was angered by the fact that some white men were "having relations" with African American women. He demanded that the police put a stop to this activity, or he would "burn the city to the ground." He did not offer any suggestions on just how he thought the police could accomplish this. As you can imagine, the letter was dismissed as a prank, and nothing was done. No one seemed worried.

The letters kept coming. Now they were sent through the mail to the jail, the Tampa Police Department and the Hillsborough County sheriff's office. Still no direct action was taken, although officials did speak out against interracial relationships. After all, what more could they do? Then the fires began. Over the next two months, over fifty fires (perhaps as many as one hundred) were set by the unknown arsonist. Most of the fires did only minor damage, but one blaze completed destroyed the original building of the Centro Asturiano, one of the early social clubs. It was that fire that earned the culprit the name of the "Ybor City Firebug."

The police became desperate. They had no name or even a good description to go on. In fact, some witnesses insisted that the arsonist was a woman, albeit a very ugly one. Despite the dearth of information, they began to make arrests anyway. Several people were brought in for questioning but then released for lack of evidence.

Things became much worse in August. On the ninth, a woman of both white and African American descent was shot while sitting on her own

Centro Asturiano club at 1915 Nebraska Avenue. *Courtesy Tampa-Hillsborough Public Library System.*

porch. She was not seriously hurt, receiving only a wound to her foot. But it became apparent that the antics of the "Ybor City Firebug" were escalating. On August 11, it happened again, and another woman of mixed descent was shot on her own porch. Her wounds were more serious than those in the first shooting, but she, too, survived. Oddly, both women were named Ada.

A few days later, police received another anonymous letter. The writer stated that he was the Firebug and that he was responsible for the recent shootings. He also said he was the man who had committed all the murders that had occurred on Christmas Eve and in early 1912. Over the next month and a half, three more women were shot and wounded.

In September, the unknown assailant shot at a police officer, yelling that he was going to murder him. He missed the officer, who turned and gave chase and was, at last, able to come up with a description of the suspect. Based on the description, more arrests were made. And those men were as quickly released as the earlier suspects.

On September 26, another woman was shot in her own home. This time the wound was instantly fatal. On October 3, another woman was killed when shots were fired through the window of her home. Panic set in. But two days later, the police spotted a man who fit the description in Ybor City. He was questioned briefly, but he appeared to be innocent. However, he gave permission for his room at a local tenement house to be searched. During that search, he slipped away and escaped custody, still in handcuffs. His name was Robert Anderson, and he was now the prime suspect—and with good reason. The police found a gun in that rented room with bullets that matched those used at one of the murders. And they found women's clothing in a large enough size to fit a man. So Anderson was also the "ugly woman" who had been seen at some of the fires.

Quickly, a massive manhunt was organized throughout the state and a reward of $2,000, an enormous amount for that day, was offered. Robert Anderson was captured in far-off Jacksonville, Florida, in November and brought back to Tampa to stand trial. It was a short one. Several witnesses suddenly could positively identify the man for whom they could not provide a description a few months before. Anderson actually admitted to the crimes but claimed he should be found not guilty by reason of insanity. The ploy did not work, and he was sentenced to death by hanging.

By all accounts, he went calmly to his death on November 22, wearing a black suit, white shirt and a black tie. Less than one year had elapsed since that first murder on Christmas Eve. Justice was swift and ruthless in those days. When the trapdoor on the scaffold was released, Anderson's neck did not break immediately, and his heart continued to beat for eight very long minutes before he was finally declared dead. Certainly it was a slow and painful death. But Ybor City could relax again, at last.

There are some who believe the Firebug still walks along Seventh Avenue. People have glimpsed, out of the corner of their eyes, an African American man dressed in a black suit, white shirt and black tie. This draws attention because it is unusual to see such formal attire in Ybor City today. When people turn to look more closely at the person they thought they saw, he has vanished. But in his wake, he has left the strong smell of wood smoke. Sometimes a large, unattractive woman has been glimpsed shuffling along. She, too, carries the strong smell of smoke with her. Those who have seen her close up report that she is quite unattractive and has a mustache. Again, if approached or questioned, she vanishes. Since the two apparitions have never been seen at the same time, it seems that Robert Anderson still likes to appear as himself sometimes and in disguise at others.

VICTOR LICATA

The insanity plea worked out a bit better for another Ybor City man in the 1930s. His story begins on an October day in 1933 in the home he shared with his family. The Licatas were prosperous and well respected. The father, Michael, owned two very successful barbershops. And the rest of the family—mother, daughter, three sons and the family dog—seemed happy on the surface. But that pleasant demeanor hid a dark secret. The eldest boy, Victor, was struggling with a mental illness so severe that it had been recommended to the family that he be committed. But they insisted that they could handle his illness and could care for him better than anyone else. They were wrong.

On October 16, Victor had spent the evening in the back of a friend's truck as they drove around town drinking moonshine. There may or may not have also been marijuana involved. Reports on that differ. He returned home around 9:00 p.m. He went right to bed and, according to his own testimony, fell sound asleep. His account of what happened next is horrifying. Victor said he woke from a sound sleep a few hours later, when his father ran into his room, grabbed him by the throat and threw him up against a wall. The rest of the family then came into the room. His brothers and sister jeered and pointed, laughing at him. Then his mother took a kitchen knife and sawed his arms off, replacing them with wooden arms with metal claws for hands. After the attack was over, Victor felt the need for revenge and found a "funny" axe—not solid but flexible, almost as if it were made of rubber—and with it, he knocked each of his family members unconscious. He then took the axe and wrung the blood out of it, the way you would wring water out of a rag. Police would later say that Victor told them this story in all seriousness, as if he believed it to be absolutely true. But Victor's arms and hands were normal and still firmly attached to his body. And his family had not been knocked unconscious. They had been hacked to death, with a very real, very inflexible axe.

The grisly scene in the house was like something out of a horror story. Michael Licata, the father, lay on the bed in the front room, killed with one blow of the axe. In one of the bedrooms lay Providence, the only daughter, and José, the youngest brother, only eight years old. It had taken many blows, but both were clearly dead. In the bedroom at the rear was the mother, Rosalie, also dead, and the middle brother, fourteen-year-old Philip, still alive despite several wounds from the axe. He did not survive the day. Even the family dog had been attacked with the axe and had managed to crawl under the front porch to die. Because the carnage had been motivated by a dream, the papers dubbed Victor "the Dream Slayer."

As you can imagine, there was considerable outrage in the community. But there was not to be a trial. Victor was found to be insane and committed for life to the state mental hospital in Chattahoochee. He was there for almost exactly twelve years. However, on October 15, 1945, five mental patients escaped. One of them was Victor Licata. And although the other four were quickly apprehended, Victor disappeared for nearly five years.

In August 1950, Victor's cousin Phillip was at work at the restaurant he owned in New Orleans. Imagine his horror when he looked up to see Victor, the man who had annihilated his own family with an axe, strolling in as if he hadn't a care in the world. Phillip remained calm and offered his cousin dinner, and they drank a few beers at a nearby bar. When they parted company, Phillip told Victor he should come back and visit him at the restaurant again the following day.

"I was afraid of him, all right, the way you'd be afraid of any crazy man," Phillip would later say. "I decided I'd get him to come back the next day and I'd have the police waiting for him."

Victor returned twice more, the following day and the day after. On that last day, Phillip grabbed his cousin, who was quite a small man, around five feet, eight inches and 127 pounds, and pinned him down until the police could arrive. Victor was temporarily housed in the Florida State Prison in Raiford, waiting for a court to decide his fate. But once again, Victor took matters into his own hands. He hanged himself with the bedsheets in his cell in December 1950.

But the question that haunts everyone to this day is "Why?" What made this quiet young man go so berserk that he murdered his entire family? There is some controversy that still lingers around this case. The truth? According to official court records from the time of his original commitment, Victor suffered from a form of dementia. And it ran in the family. There is evidence that his fourteen-year-old brother, Phillip, suffered from the same disorder. Victor also had an uncle and two cousins who suffered so severely from mental problems that they had to be committed to asylums. It is also true that Victor's parents were first cousins. So the most likely cause of his delirium was a genetic mental disease.

However, there are always those who don't want to let the truth get in the way of a good story. In 1930, a man named Henry Anslinger was appointed by President Herbert Hoover to head a new branch of the U.S. government, the Federal Bureau of Narcotics. Anslinger was in need of the job. He had been assistant commissioner for the Bureau of Prohibition, and Prohibition was about to come to an end.

Anslinger was a zealot who believed that Prohibition would have been successful if only the penalties had been harsher. Now that alcohol was legal again, he turned his attentions to a new substance he wanted banned: marijuana. In 1934, he began a media campaign against it. There are some who say his motives were highly suspect. It has been alleged that he was helping the DuPont chemical interests and William Randolph Hearst. Dupont and Hearst wanted hemp products eliminated because hemp was an effective competitor against their chemical and paper interests. However, it is doubtful that Anslinger would have needed much convincing, as his own opinions were quite strong—and quite racist.

One of the reasons he though marijuana should be criminalized was because of its supposed effect on "the degenerate races." He insisted that smoking marijuana made "darkies think they're as good as white men" and made white women "seek sexual relations with Negros, entertainers, and any others." Obviously he also held entertainers in low regard. He believed the entire development of jazz music was due to the smoking of marijuana. Most people would see the development of jazz as a good thing, but Anslinger was not one of them.

With support from William Randolph Hearst, which is suspicious to say the least, Anslinger began writing for the *American Magazine*. He developed what became known as the "Gore File," in which he collected horrendous crimes that had been perpetrated under the influence of "Reefer Madness." He wrote:

> *An entire family was murdered by a youthful addict in Florida. When officers arrive*[d] *at the home, they found the youth staggering about in a human slaughterhouse. With an ax he had killed his father, mother, two brothers and a sister. He seemed to be in a daze…He had no recollection of having committed the multiple crime*[s]. *The officers knew him ordinarily as a sane, rather quiet young man; now he was pitifully crazed. The*[y] *sought the reason. They* [s]*aid* [that] *he had been in the habit of smoking something which youthful friends called "muggles," a childish name for marijuana.*

Sound familiar? Of course he was referring to the Licata murders, but he got many of the facts wrong. The Tampa police, in fact, knew Victor to be deeply disturbed, not a "quiet young man," and in all the court records regarding the commitment hearings, marijuana was never mentioned. In fact, nearly all the roughly two hundred cases in Anslinger's Gore File have now been discredited. It turned out that marijuana was actually not involved in most of the cases. And for some of the cases, no one can find any evidence that they even really occurred. Unbelievably, this bigoted fanatic remained in his position of head of the Bureau of Narcotics until 1962, when he finally retired at the age of seventy. He died 1975.

The legend of the ghost of Victor Licata has grown over the years. Some believe that his spirit returns to the scene of the crime, his family home on Fifth Avenue in Ybor City, where he wanders the rooms, looking for his lost parents and siblings. Sounds of his crying and the screams of his victims can be heard in the early hours each morning. However, neither the current owner nor the one before her have reported any such occurrences in the house. It is hoped that after all these years, the tortured soul of Victor Licata now rests in peace.

CHARLIE WALL

The large white house still stands. It looks out of place in a neighborhood that has definitely seen better days. Butterflies fly around the large yard, and all looks peaceful. But this was the site of a grisly murder. And the murder victim was a criminal himself. In a way he was the "King of Tampa" in the 1920s and 1930s. His name was Charlie Wall.

Charlie Wall during his testimony for the Organized Crime Committee. *Courtesy of Ybor City State Museum.*

Charles Wall was born in 1880. His father was John P. Wall, an eminent physician and a mayor of Tampa, who discovered the cause of yellow fever. His mother was Matilda McKay, a member of one of the richest families in Florida. One would think that Charlie would have had a childhood with all the advantages that money and social position could buy. But things began to go very badly for Charles when he reached his teenage years. In 1893, his mother passed away. It was less than six months later that

Dr. John married his housekeeper, Louise Williams. Charlie hated his stepmother. He would later say that she was a cruel woman who spent his father's money too freely. Things went from bad to worse when John himself died in 1895, leaving the custody of his young son in the hands of the "wicked stepmother." Louise's spending habits became even worse without the steadying influence of John, and Charlie grew to dislike her more and more. He began spending more and more time away from home, often in bad company at the saloons, brothels and gambling parlors. Things finally came to a head when he shot his stepmother with a .22-caliber rifle. "I was just tired of her," he later explained. Despite being wounded, Louise did survive. But as you can imagine, she wanted nothing to do with her wayward stepson.

After a short stay in juvenile detention, Charlie was packed off to Birmingham Military School in North Carolina. He didn't stay there long, as he was quickly expelled. He would later claim that he had been gambling and hanging around in brothels and was thrown out for this flaunting of the rules. However, school records indicate that he was expelled for the more mundane transgression of cheating on a test. For whatever reason, his military career was over. He returned to Tampa, but he did not go back to the stepmother he hated (and it was doubtful that she wanted him back anyway after he shot her). Instead, he began living on the streets of Ybor City and learning the ways of the criminal element. He was dealing craps in illegal casinos in the red-light district before he reached his sixteenth birthday. He was a very successful gambler himself because he was a mathematical whiz bordering on a genius.

In the early twentieth century, Charlie used his knowledge of mathematical probabilities to take over the numbers racket in Ybor City. Known as "bolita" or "little ball," it was a very popular (although illegal) lottery-style game. Much like today's perfectly legal Powerball lottery game, bolita involved placing bets on which numbers would be drawn from a large group of balls. In the case of bolita, numbers from one to one hundred were written on small balls made of wood or ivory. The balls were then drawn from cloth bags. With his skill at numbers, Charlie was perfectly capable of making a profit on a totally honest game. However, he was not above rigging the odds when it suited him. Sometimes, he would put lead weights in the balls carrying numbers he did not want to be drawn. These balls would then sink to the bottom of the bolita bag and be much less likely to be pulled out. Also, if there were a number he wanted to be drawn, Charlie would have that ball frozen. It was easy for the man Charlie had appointed to pull a "cold one" out of the bag. Charles would remain in control of bolita for the next twenty-five years.

With his profits, Charlie branched out into other traditional areas of organized crime: drugs, prostitution and, during Prohibition, illegal alcohol. Ironically, his upper-class background helped him in many ways. As a son of both the prominent Wall family and the wealthy McKay family, doors were open to him that were not open to the average hoodlum. He could go to country clubs, fine restaurants and homes of the wealthy. And even the influential and wealthy loved to play bolita. He also knew how to dress and act the part. He dressed like a gentleman, in a white-linen suit, and his manner was described as polite and soft-spoken.

In 1910, Charlie consolidated his power with the working class of Tampa and Ybor by supporting the cigar workers' strike. This was more than lip service on his part, as he paid medical and food bills for those who were struggling. And although the strike was not successful, those workers never forgot Charlie Wall. He became their hero. They supported him, and more importantly, they voted the way he wanted them to vote. This helped Charlie gain control of the politicians, judges and city leaders throughout the 1910s, '20s and '30s. Not only did officials leave Charlie's operations alone, but also if someone else set himself up as a potential rival, his operations were quickly raided by the police, who were firmly in Charlie's pocket. Charlie was Tampa's version of a "Teflon Don." Although he was brought to trial on a few occasions, he was always acquitted. Rivals who were being squeezed out of their "piece of the pie" tried to have him assassinated, but he always survived.

On one memorable occasion, Charlie was facing certain death, as two hit men had his car pinned in. His driver, "Baby Joe," who also often served as a bodyguard, stood on the car's running board. While still driving with one hand and firing his gun with the other, he maneuvered the car backward through traffic. Neither Joe nor Charlie had so much as a scratch.

Charlie was often asked how he escaped so many attempts on his life. His reply was, "The devil looks after his own."

As the 1930s wore on, Charlie began to tire of his dangerously exciting life. By 1940, he had retired and moved to Miami, leaving a blood bath behind, as other racketeers tried to grab a hunk of Charlie's power.

That could have been the end of the story, but something happened in 1950 that changed everything. That year, Tennessee senator Estes Kefauver, who had aspirations of becoming president, saw the issue of organized crime as his ticket to the White House. On May 3, he became head of the "Special

Committee to Investigate Crime in Interstate Commerce." This committee held hearings in fourteen major cities across the United States, including Tampa. Many prominent gangland figures were called to testify. All of them denied any connection with organized crime—all, that is, except Charlie Wall, who returned from Miami to testify. To use gangster vernacular, Charlie "sang like a canary." He gave details, told secrets and named names. Accounts of the time say that he captivated the whole city with his dry wit and intriguing tales. The hearings played on live television throughout the country, and Charlie became a celebrity.

Enjoying his renewed fame in the city of his birth, Charlie moved back to Tampa, where he continued to entertain and thrill with his stories of his life of crime. This was not very smart. Many of those in power were not happy about either Charlie's testimony at the hearings or his return to Tampa. Even though he had no real power anymore, he was seen as a threat. He was warned by his friends to keep quiet and lay low. But it appears he was just having too much fun with his notoriety, and once again, he survived several attempts on his life. Apparently, the devil was still looking after his own.

But on an April night in 1955, the devil must have had better things to do. It appears that Charlie had opened the door for someone he knew and trusted, as there was no forced entry into his home. His wife, who had been out of town, found his body the next morning. He was wearing his pajamas and a dressing gown. He had been beaten about the head with a sock filled with birdseed, which actually makes a formidable weapon and is a traditional mark of disrespect for someone who "sang" to the authorities. The assailants also used a baseball bat, and Charlie's throat had been slit from ear to ear. On the nightstand next to Charlie's bed was a copy of *Crime in America* by Estes Kefauver. Had Charlie been reading it before he opened the door to his attackers? Or did the perpetrators leave it there as a warning to any others who might be tempted to "sing?"

Who murdered Charlie Wall? To this day, no one knows. The police did have a few suspects, but the murder remains unsolved. And an unsolved murder seems one of the primary causes for a haunting.

And Charlie does still seem to find his old "haunts," mostly in downtown Tampa. His white-suited figure has been seen in Oaklawn Cemetery, where he is buried; in the Sapphire Room at the Hotel Floridan, where he loved to drink with his pals; and on the street in between. But his ghost is most closely associated with the Old Federal Courthouse, just a bit farther down Florida Avenue—perhaps because it was in that building that the Kefauver hearings were held and where he first told the stories that ultimately led to his death.

Passersby who have photographed the steps of the courthouse after nightfall have seen strange things in their images. Bright orange lights appeared in the transoms of the huge glass doors on the main level. Misty faces have been seen in the windows of the upper stories. The most eerie of all was an image of a figure in white mist that seemed to be descending the staircase. Perhaps this is the most appropriate of all, since one of Charlie's nicknames during his reign as the king of Tampa's underworld was the "White Shadow." Paul Guzzo said in his documentary about Charlie Wall, "In real life, sometimes the bad guys wear white."

The Old Federal Courthouse, which was built in 1905, has recently been converted to a beautiful Le Meridien Hotel. The developers made use of some of the grand details of the old building. Perhaps in the future they will have some tales of the ghost of Charlie Wall to share with us.

But old Charlie certainly haunts the streets of Ybor City as well. Look for him in the local bars, on the streets near the social clubs and at the El Pasaje building, which was the site of the old Cherokee Club, one of Charlie's favorite places. He will be easy to recognize. Just look for the white suit, the straw hat and, of course, that "extra smile," where his throat was slit from ear to ear. Remember to show proper respect to the ghost of the former "King of Tampa."

Chapter 4
REBELS AND RADICALS

JOSÉ MARTÍ

Cuba Libre! Freedom for Cuba. Liberate Cuba. This cause was very dear to the heart of many a Cuban living in Ybor City, including Don Vicente Martínez de Ybor himself. He left Cuba to begin manufacturing fine cigars in the United States because Cuban authorities knew he was working for the cause of Cuban freedom from the colonial rule of Spain. The exiled Cuban community wanted to contribute to the struggle in their homeland. And they found just the hero to help them do that. His name was José Martí.

José Julian Martí Pérez was born in Havana, Cuba, on January 28, 1853. His family moved to Spain when he was only four years old, but they moved back to Cuba two years later. José went to the public school, and education was very important to him and to his family. He was deeply affected by the assassination of Abraham Lincoln. Even at the tender age of thirteen, he became vehemently opposed to colonial rule and slavery, which was still being practiced in Cuba at the time. But the Spanish government was tightening its grip on the island, coming down hard on even minor forms of dissent. When José was sixteen, a friend of his joined the Spanish army. José wrote this friend a scathing letter reproving him for working on behalf of Spain. Somehow this letter came to the attention of the authorities, and José was charged with treason. He was held in jail for four months, until he "confessed" to the charges. It is likely that this so-called confession was coerced through rough treatment and the conditions of his incarceration. Even though he was still a minor and his sole crime was writing a letter to a friend, he was sentenced to six years in prison. His treatment in prison did not improve. Eventually he became very ill from an infection that was the result of his legs being severely lacerated by the chains used to bind him. Finally, when he was eighteen, he was deported from Cuba to Spain. He was then allowed to continue his education. The authorities hoped that if he lived in Spain for a few years, he would lose his sympathy for Cuban independence. They were wrong. His horrible treatment only served to strengthen his resolve to bring about the freedom of the land where he was born.

Although he became a real renaissance man—poet, essayist, journalist and publisher (he even published a magazine for children)—his true passion was always *Cuba Libre*. He spent the rest of his life traveling on both sides of the Atlantic, raising money and recruiting converts for his favorite cause.

His travels brought him to Ybor City for the first time in 1891. He so inspired the Cuban exiles in Florida that for the next six years, they worked and raised funds for Cuban independence. Some pledged part of their weekly pay—sometimes as much as one whole day's pay each week. Others sold jewelry and other valuables to contribute money to the cause. This dedication seemed to temporarily diminish what had been a growing tension between owners and workers. Everyone was pulling together.

But Spanish authorities in Cuba had other ideas about José Martí. During José's visit to Ybor City in November 1892, their agents attempted to poison him. The poison was put into his wine glass, but he must have noticed a strange taste for he immediately vomited the poison and suffered no ill effects. The attempt on his life only gained him greater sympathy among the Cubans in Ybor City. It was at that time that he became friends with Ruperto and Paulina Pedroso, an Afro-Cuban couple. From then on, he stayed in their home. Paulina would personally taste everything he ate or drank to prevent future episodes of poisoning. Ruperto would sleep sitting up on a chair outside José's room with a shotgun over his knees. And the couple's sons would sleep outside under José's window. He came to Ybor City twenty documented times and perhaps more. He always stayed with the Pedrosos, with whom he was safe. Such was the power of his personality and oratory that the two men who had tried to poison him later came to him, confessed their crime and begged his forgiveness, which he willingly gave. They became dedicated fighters for Cuban liberation.

The steps of the front entrance to Ybor's brick factory building. These are a reproduction paid for by the Republic of Cuba after the original steps were taken to Cuba because José Martí had spoken on them. *Author's collection.*

After much preparation, José returned to Cuba in 1895. There he made contact with the Cuban rebels and in the Battle of Dos Ríos, he was killed while leading an ill-fated charge. He was wearing a black jacket and riding a white horse and made an easy target. He is buried in Cementerio Santa Ifigenia in Santiago de Cuba. His revolution did not succeed until the entry of the United States into the war in 1898.

It is impossible to overstate the importance of José Martí to the Cuban people. Rodney Kite-Powell of the Tampa Historical Society says, "José Martí is really Cuba's Abraham Lincoln and George Washington rolled into one." They call him the "Apostle of Freedom," and to this day, both Castro's communist government and the Cuban community in exile, who fled that very government, claim José Martí as their inspiration and hero.

In the 1950s, before Castro, the Cuban government visited Ybor City. It discovered that Martí had made a speech on the iron steps of Don Ybor's cigar factory. It officially requested to remove those steps and take them to Cuba. When permission was granted, the government took the steps but replaced the ones on the factory with an exact replica.

Statue of José Martí in the Friends of José Martí Park, which is Cuban soil. *Author's collection.*

Another very interesting transfer took place that involved the house where Martí so often stayed. Ruperto and Paulina Pedroso returned to a liberated Cuba in 1910 and sold their property in Ybor City. It passed through several hands, and it was not well kept up or cared for. In 1951, it was purchased by a couple in Havana who wanted to establish a memorial to José Martí. At first they wanted to disassemble the house itself and move it to Cuba. But it was too damaged by dry rot and termites to survive. So instead, the house was torn down, and the land became the Parque Amigos de José Martí, or "Friends of José Martí Park." What many people don't know is that the money to establish the park was donated by Fulgencio Batista, who was president of Cuba from 1940 to 1944 and again from 1952 to 1959. In 1956, the property was officially transferred to the Republic of Cuba. Yes, this small park is Cuban soil. Every day people walk by, not realizing that if they would just walk through the iron gate, they would have traveled to Cuba without benefit of passport or visa.

Parque Amigos de José Martí is located at 1303 Eighth Avenue. But perhaps it is not the best place to visit after dark, for several spirits seem to linger in the park. There are several distinct voices heard speaking Spanish, including a man's voice lifted in inspiring oratory. Perhaps José has returned to Ybor City in death. Is he still trying to raise funds and recruits to free Cuba from tyranny? How does he truly feel about the current regime in his native island? A woman's voice is also heard, but she is soft-spoken. Perhaps the ghost of Paulina has returned to the spot where she and her family once protected their hero. Besides the voices, there are some who claim that the statue of José Martí has been seen to change position slightly, particularly his outstretched hand moves up or down. Perhaps he is adding emphasis to his words with gestures, even to this day.

THE STRIKES

The unity between workers and factory owners that was apparent during the years of the Cuban Independence movement soon faded. The workers wanted the usual things: more pay, better working conditions, better hours. They also were very concerned about mechanization. Could the skilled workers who hand rolled the cigars be replaced? Could fine cigars be made by machine? They soon banded together into unions, just as they had in New York and Key West.

The owners had their concerns as well. They were facing competition from the much less expensive cigarettes and cheap machine-made cigars. They were feeling the pressure to modernize operations. With these two competing goals and visions, labor strikes were inevitable.

Although there was a brief walk out by Spanish workers in 1887, it was due to a clash over Cubans versus Spaniards. It was more about nationalities than labor relations. The first real strike occurred in 1889. It lasted ninety-eight days. It was all about the use of scales to weigh the tobacco given to each worker at the beginning of the day. The workers were used to rolling and smoking cigars for themselves during the day. They viewed the weighing of tobacco as an end to this important privilege of the job. Ultimately, the workers returned to their rolling tables.

Original Labor Temple at 1612 Eighth Avenue with a crowd on the street. *Courtesy Tampa-Hillsborough Public Library System.*

The strike of 1900 lasted forty-two days and was also basically over the issue of the workers' making cigars for themselves. A compromise was reached. A worker could still make cigars for his own use, but no more than three a day. This practice is still used today in the cigar industry.

The strike of 1901 lasted only one day. It was specifically designed as a protest over the closing of a bridge that made it difficult to get from one side of the river to the other. The mayor of Tampa promised to open the bridge as soon as possible, and indeed it did reopen twenty-one days later.

The list of such strikes is very long. And in the end, modernization won out, which in turn caused the decline of Ybor City's cigar industry. But violence along the way created some interesting hauntings.

In 1902, the struggle was over the *lector*. It started off simply enough. One of the factories, Bustillo Brothers and Díaz, which was actually located in West Tampa, informed the president of the committee that collected the money for the *lectores*' pay that he could not do the collecting inside the

M. Pérez Cigar Factory. *Courtesy Tampa-Hillsborough Public Library System.*

factory but must take care of that matter on the street outside. The reader at that time was Francisco Milian. He was so well respected that he had been elected mayor of West Tampa (a separate city from Tampa proper). He viewed the collecting of his pay in the public street as a personal insult and quit his job immediately. The workers, who respected Milian as much for his role as their reader as for his mayorship, went on strike in his support. And it wasn't just those at Bustillo Brothers—most workers from the factories in both Ybor City and West Tampa walked out, too.

The reaction of the factory owners was swift and harsh. They hired thugs, who kidnapped Milian, took him to a remote wooded area, stripped him, beat him nearly to death and then offered him the choice of leaving the country and going back to Cuba or immediate execution if he stayed in Florida. And this man was the mayor of West Tampa at the time! He did choose exile over death, but when news of this circulated among the workers, more of them joined the strike. Once Milian heard about the massive support from the workers, he became determined to return. Upon his arrival in Ybor City, he was greeted with a hero's welcome. Over two thousand cheering supporters met him at the train station and continued to cheer him as he made a speech at the Labor Temple. After this speech, the Cigar Makers Union demanded that he be restored to his former position. The factory owners gave in on the question, and the strike was ended. So the workers won this round.

The actual building where Milian made his famous speech stood at 1612 Eighth Avenue. It was torn down in the 1920s. But on that old corner, those who pass by have heard voices. The voices seem to be cheering, although the sound is muffled, as if coming from far away. Those who are sensitive to such things have also said that there is a definite feeling of anger and defiance at that spot. The feeling is so strong at times that it seems overwhelming. This particular type of haunting would not be that of an intelligent spirit, able to interact with the present, but a residual type, in which the energy from the past remains and seems to repeat in an endless loop.

Violence reached its peak during the strike of 1910. It began in June and lasted well into the fall. Perhaps the Florida heat made matters worse, for tempers seemed very short. There were many beatings, shootings and deportations. The culmination of the disorder also involved the Bustillo Brothers and Díaz Factory. On September 14, a bookkeeper (considered part of management) named Easterling was shot by assailants unknown. He later died of his wounds. On September 21, two Italian men, Castange Ficcarrotta and Angelo Albano, were arrested and charged with the shooting. There was absolutely no evidence that these were the two who were guilty. Neither of them were leaders in the labor movement. In fact, only one of them was even a member of the union. For the owners, that didn't matter. It was more a matter of having someone to be a scapegoat and use as an example. That evening, a mob of around sixty people, most likely hired by the factory owners, confronted the police escort as the prisoners were being transferred to the Hillsborough County jail and abducted the two Italians. The next morning, their bodies were found hanging from a tree on one of the main thoroughfares in Tampa (now Kennedy Boulevard). According to the coroner's report, Albano had been shot in the stomach prior to his actual death, and both men had broken necks, which would have been the cause of death. Attached to the foot of one of the hanging bodies was found the following note: "Beware! Others take notice or go the same way! We are watching you!"

Although the newspapers at the time seemed to think that justice had been served by the lynching, there is no reason to believe that was the case. The assessment of Gaetano Moroni, the Italian vice-counsel in New Orleans, is probably the most accurate—that the whole thing was planned in advance by some of the factory owners with the "tacit assent of a few police officers."

The two were buried almost immediately in Woodlawn Cemetery just outside the boundaries of Ybor City. The families of both men were in attendance, and they were sobbing and overcome with grief. To this day, the sound of their sobbing is heard near the graves of Ficcarrotta and Albano, another residual haunting.

The wave of violence did not abate. More horrible acts were committed throughout Ybor City after the lynching. The hatred between both sides grew. The factories reopened in October, but many workers did not return until things finally began to settle down in November. (This is also the strike during which Charlie Wall gave a great deal of money to workers to help them through the rough times. This laid the foundation for his control of the city in the subsequent decades.)

Although there were a few strikes after this, the spirit of the unions had effectively been broken, and the decline of Ybor City as the Cigar Capital of the world became inevitable.

Chapter 5

SOCIAL CLUBS

Ybor City was a new town, founded out of the wilderness on the edge of the small, frontier village of Tampa. No one who came there had been born in Ybor City because it had just come into existence. Nearly all of them were born outside the state of Florida. And most of them had been born outside the boundaries of the United States. They brought with them their languages and cultures and wanted to preserve them. The people who settled here were not just separate from the mainly white culture of Tampa but also, in some respects, even separate from one another within what came to be know as the "Latin Community." This term encompasses those who came from Cuba, Italy and Spain. To this end, they formed "social clubs," where they could mingle with people who shared their values and spoke their language with their accent.

But the social clubs became so much more. They evolved into mutual aid societies, much like fraternal organizations. Members paid weekly dues and received in return, free medical care, entertainment and education. Tampa historian Gary Mormino said, "If the cigar factories functioned as the economic heart of Ybor City, surely the mutual aid societies served as its soul." The buildings erected by these social clubs are some of the most beautiful in Tampa, not just Ybor City. Mr. Mormino calls them "cathedrals of the working class." And most, but not all, of these buildings, have the reputation of being haunted.

EL CENTRO ESPAÑOL (SPANISH CLUB)

This club was the first one to be formed, organizing on December 21, 1891. According to Ignacio Haya, the first club president, the purpose of the club was "first to unite the Spanish colony in Tampa and secondly to create a center for her recreation and instruction." It cost $16,000 to build the group's first clubhouse, which was a wood-frame building at Seventh Avenue and Sixteenth Street. From the beginning, the club offered courses in English for both children and adults as well as a meeting place. At first medical benefits were not provided, but when members soon saw the need for them, those programs were started. Interestingly enough, you did not have to have been born in Spain to become a member; you could simply be of Spanish descent.

The red brick edifice that now stands at the 1526–1536 Seventh Avenue was completed in 1912 to replace the old clubhouse, which had been destroyed by fire. When it was built it contained a theater, classrooms, a dance hall, a canteen and a soda fountain. The third-floor ballroom had a

Interior of Centro Español with men at tables playing cards. *Courtesy Tampa-Hillsborough Public Library System.*

The Spanish Club building today. *Author's collection.*

balcony for an orchestra. The club disbanded in 1983, and today, the elegant structure houses several offices as well as a restaurant, the Carne Chophouse. The servers at the chop house report that they have a problem with candles in the restaurant. At the end of the evening, they will make sure all the candles have been extinguished as they finish closing the restaurant for the night. Often, the candles reignite themselves, causing staff members to have to go over and make sure they are all snuffed completely out. However, when they look back a few moments later, the candles have lit themselves again. Is this being done by the spirit of one of the long-ago members, who just wants to keep the party going? In other parts of the building, it has been reported that the sound of a baby crying is heard when there is no infant anywhere near the vicinity. This is most often experienced in the stairwell leading to the upper floors and in the women's restroom on the upper level. Recently, a woman visiting the old clubhouse needed the restroom. While she was washing her hands, she heard the sound of a baby crying in the hallway, as if in great distress. Being somewhat concerned, she hurried out in the hallway to see if she could assist a parent who needed help. As soon as she left the rest room, the crying stopped abruptly, and there was absolutely no one in the wide hallway or on the stairs. Again, we have no idea whose child might

The Spanish Club in the 1940s. *Courtesy of Ybor City State Museum.*

be making the racket. Perhaps it is the spirit of a child who accompanied a parent to the club for a meeting and simply wanted attention—and is still wanting attention, even after all these years.

The club also had a clinic building on Fifteenth Street, known as La Beneficia. That building has been put to several uses over the years. In 1997, it was turned into the Sugar Palm Ballroom, and it had a brief life as a "swing dance" club, closing in 1999. However, dancers frequently reported seeing a ghostly figure dressed in 1930s garb moving through the crowd. Could this have been someone who died in the old clinic and was brought back by hearing the music of his own era once again? In 2003, the building was turned into a studio for the dance program for Hillsborough Community College. During the renovation, workers complained that they were being harassed by an unknown entity. Could this same gentleman have returned to express his dissatisfaction that the music and dancers were no longer there? Since the dance studio opened there have been no further reports of ghostly activity.

L'UNION ITALIANA (ITALIAN CLUB)

This club is still in existence, and where it once taught English to Italians, it now teaches Italian to English speakers. The club has a website and a newsletter. It is firmly part of the twenty-first century, but its roots go back to the nineteenth. Begun in 1894, it was formed to benefit Italians from all over the entire city. The weekly dues included the usual social events and medical care but also came to include funerals and burials as the Italian Club maintains its cemetery to this day. The first permanent clubhouse was appropriately dedicated on Columbus Day in 1912. But it only stood for three years before one of the many fires in Ybor City destroyed it. The Italian Renaissance–style building that now stands was completed in 1917. There was a theater, a dance floor, a cantina, a bowling alley, recreational and educational rooms and a library. The Italian Club became famous for its dances. Sometimes two bands would play in the same evening.

The stories of haunting here are less prevalent than at the Spanish Club. But there is one story. A cleaning woman has been seen on the stairway, down on her knees with a scrub bucket and brush. Her hairstyle, her clothing and her method of cleaning seem to belong to a different era than today's. If she is approached, she will look up and smile, as if she is completely at home. If you ask her name, she will say, "Virginia" and then vanish right in front of your eyes.

The Italian Club has been a popular place for paranormal investigators. One group was using an EVP recorder on the stairway. This is actually a regular digital recorder, but it is allowed to run while the investigator asked questions, leaving pauses for the answer. Later, the paranormal analyst listened very carefully to the recording. In this particular case, the investigator had asked, "Is your name Virginia?" The answer, not heard by normal hearing, was clearly audible on the digital device: "Yes."

Another investigation made use of a different ghost-hunting tool, the K2 EMF meter. This device measures electromagnetic fields. Although these fields can be produced by electrical interference, it is believed that a spirit can manipulate the lights and dials on these meters to give answers to "yes" or "no" questions. A group of young women believed that they made contact with a woman in one of the ladies' rooms. The spirit told the girls that she was seventy years old and that she had two sons, a grandson and a daughter-in-law she didn't like. When a male entered the room, the communication stopped abruptly. As they were leaving the ladies room, the motion activated paper towel dispenser whirred as it spat out a paper towel.

Dancers in the Italian Club ballroom in the 1920s. *Courtesy of Ybor City State Museum.*

No one was anywhere near the device. At the same time, another member of the team was "talking" with the spirit of a young boy at the bar.

None of the people who have experienced hauntings in the Ybor City Italian Club have felt frightened in any way. The ghosts here, they all affirm, are only of the friendly kind.

CENTRO ASTURIANO (ASTURIAN CLUB)

Asturias is a mountainous region in Spain. Despite opposition from the Spanish Club, already functioning, the immigrants to Ybor City from this region wanted to start their own social club. There already existed a Centro Asturiano in Havana, and the men who came from Cuba to Florida wanted to continue that tradition. The main purpose of this club was medical and death benefits. It founded a hospital, as well as a cemetery.

Centro Asturiano Hospital, showing the archway in the lobby. *Courtesy Tampa-Hillsborough Public Library System.*

The hospital was the most important part of the club. In the 1930s, it had seventy beds, a pharmacy, six doctors and seven nurses. It was considered the most modern and well-equipped facility in the city of Tampa. But the hospital did not keep up with the times after World War II, and it was closed permanently in 1990. After the closing of the hospital, membership declined precipitously. Although the club continues to function in its beautiful building on Nebraska Avenue, it really serves only a social and historical function. The facilities are available for rental for private parties and wedding receptions, which help to keep the club afloat. There have been no reports of ghosts at the Centro Asturiano…so far.

THE GERMAN AMERICAN CLUB

As time moved on, Ybor City began to welcome people from lands other than Spain, Cuba or Italy. By the dawn of the twentieth century, there were enough people of German background to want their own club. These German immigrants were not cigar makers. They had backgrounds in business, and they mainly worked in the organizational part of cigar manufacturing as managers, bookkeepers and supervisors. The club had a very short life, as it went out of existence just before World War I. Due to the ill feeling against Germany during the war, many German residents moved back to Europe. There are no hauntings associated with the German American Club. Perhaps it wasn't around long enough to have a ghost. The beautiful building still stands at 2105 Nebraska Avenue. It is currently city property and serves as the Ybor Service Center.

SOCIEDAD MARTÍ–MACEO (MARTÍ–MACEO SOCIETY CLUB)

Although Afro-Cubans and white Cubans worked side by side in the factory, they had separate social clubs. Integrated clubs were actually prohibited by Florida law. Organized in 1901, the club took it name from two martyrs from the struggle for Cuban independence. The original clubhouse, a two-story wood-frame structure, was the largest secular meeting facility for persons of color in Tampa. It had a nine-hundred-seat theater, a ballroom and meeting rooms. The club is still in existence in a new space at 1226 East Seventh Avenue.

Círculo Cubano (Cuban Club)

Last, but certainly not least, is the most haunted of all the Ybor City social clubs: Circulo Cubano. In fact, the Travel Channel lists it as one of the top ten most haunted places in America. And it is number three on a website entitled "The Top Ten Haunted Places We Never Want to Visit." The Atlantic Paranormal Society (TAPS), which is featured in the television show *Ghosthunters*, produced an episode at the club entitled "Club Dead."

The Cuban Club most likely had its beginnings in the revolutionary clubs and societies formed to help Cuba gain its independence from Spain. In 1887, Vicente Martínez de Ybor himself donated a vacant factory warehouse to his Cuban workers for use as a meeting place. This first building was replaced in 1907 at a cost of $18,000. Sadly, the new building only lasted until 1916, when it fell victim to a fire in Ybor City. The building dedicated in 1918 remains standing to this day, and Circulo Cubano is still an active club.

The spirits at the Cuban Club really seem to like the piano. There have been several reports of music coming from the instrument when no one is near it. Sometimes, it isn't music but discordant noise. Krista, a former employee, shared her terrifying experience with the ghostly piano player. This occurred one evening while she was giving a tour of the stately clubhouse to a group of students from Hillsborough Community College. "The tour ran later than usual," she said. "By the time we finished everyone else had already left, so I had to turn the lights off and lock the doors." She went on to explain how, since the light switches are not near the door, she had to turn on a flashlight to make her way through the dark. Naturally, this made her feel a bit on edge in the dark old building. Suddenly she heard a loud crashing of notes, as if someone was pounding on the piano keys. Thinking she had inadvertently left one of the students behind, she went rushing to the theater, some of her tour group following behind her. When she shone her flashlight on the piano, there was no one there, but the blast of sound continued to fill the room. What was really bizarre was that the keys on the piano were actually moving, as if being depressed by an unseen hand. Krista and her group turned on their heels and got out of there fast.

Krista and her co-worker Jane would often have to remain in the Cuban Club late at night to clean up after events. Jane described an evening when she was cleaning downstairs, and Krista was upstairs. Both definitely heard a woman's voice screaming, "Help me! Help me!" Jane thought it was Krista, and Krista thought it was Jane. They both went running to find each other,

Cuban Club. Four-story Neoclassical building on Fourteenth Street. *Courtesy Tampa-Hillsborough Public Library System.*

only to discover that neither one of them had been yelling. To top it all off, as the girls were leaving that night, they met a gentleman out on Fourteenth Street, who asked them questions about the history of the club. He explained the reason for his curiosity. His grandmother had once worked there as a restroom attendant. Had this been his grandmother's voice calling out to him for help as he stood outside the Cuban Club?

Whoever she may be, the poor woman's cries have been heard on other occasions. One night, Krista was running a bit late for work. Her cellphone rang just as she pulled into the parking lot. It was the club manager, and he sounded very worried. Krista reassured him that she was almost there. But that is not why he was worried. He had heard a voice yelling, "Help me! Help me!" He had assumed it was Krista, but when he went to look for her, he could not find her—or anybody else who could have been pleading for help. He was relieved to hear that Krista was all right.

Those who stay at the club into the wee hours have noticed another strange occurrence. At around four or five o'clock in the morning, the elevators start going up and down on their own. Some of the staff believe that some sort of electrical problem is to blame, but no natural explanation has ever been found. And why would an electrical problem only occur at four or five o'clock in the morning? The staff jokingly puts the blame on the first president of the Cuban Club, Salvador Martínez. Krista also says that two portraits, one of the club's first president and one of the second president, hang in the room that contains a large old black safe. She has experienced the eyes of these paintings following her as she moves about the room. She wonders if the two long-dead gentlemen are still trying to protect the safe.

And strangest of all, there is an apparition of a man that has been seen by several people. For those who believe, there are many ways for ghosts or spirits to manifest themselves: temperature changes, sounds, electromagnetic pulses, balls of light or orbs. But the sighting of a full-blown apparition is extremely rare. Just watch any of the current crop of "ghost hunting" programs, and you will see that even people who do this for a living almost never "see a ghost." But the man at the Cuban Club has been seen by many. He wears an old-style suit and a white fedora hat. He moves very quickly, flashing by the viewer at beyond human speed. This specter leaves the strong smell of pipe tobacco in his wake. It is very interesting that in the city that was once the cigar capital of the world, the ghostly visitor smokes a pipe.

And there is even more. Gladys Garcia was executive director of the Cuban Club Foundation from September 2002 to October 2010. During her tenure, she granted an interview to a paranormal investigator and blogger. In the interview, Garcia told the story of a dancer who frequented the Cuban Club during the "Roaring Twenties." Her name was Carlita, and she died when she either jumped or was pushed from the third-floor balcony in the theater. When a psychic tried to contact the spirit of Carlita, the dancer from long ago seemed reluctant to communicate. Eventually, she confirmed that she was indeed pushed after she had spurned the advances of one of the local tough guys. She also said that at the time, she thought herself safe because she was under the protection of the local top crime boss as his mistress. Her spirit is at least pleased that revenge for her murder was swift and fitting. Within one week of her death, her killer had been "executed" by the local mob. If Carlita lived in the 1920s, then the top local crime boss would have been Charlie Wall, whom we have discussed before. Could this be the man in the white fedora who is seen in the club?

Since Charlie was not of Cuban descent, he would not have had any reason to have been in the Cuban Club, unless he was there for love or revenge, so this may not be his spirit. There are at least two other possibilities.

Gladys Garcia believes that the apparition of a man in the suit is a former club president named Albert J. Kolby, also known as *el fumador*, or "the smoker." According to Ms. Garcai, *el fumador* had been helping himself to a little too much of the club's money in 1917. There was an ugly confrontation in one of the conference rooms during which other board members accused him of embezzling. Angry words were exchanged and then one of the other board members took out a pistol and shot Kolby at point-blank range, right in the face. There have also been reports of muttering sounds being heard from the boardroom. Could this be the board members trying to decide how to confront *el fumador* regarding the Cuban Club's missing funds?

Another source names a different man in a different year. According to Tim Reeser in his book *Ghost Stories of Tampa, Florida*, a man named Bellarmino Vallejo was serving on the board of directors of the club during the 1930s. Some people were very unhappy with the way the club was being managed. An argument over finances ended in Vallejo's being shot in the face.

The two stories are so similar it is unlikely that they both occurred. If they did, serving on the board of the Cuban Club is indeed a dangerous job. There is no definitive documentation of either case. Some stories even claim that there was a woman who was shot during a heated political debate. The records of the Cuban Club now reside at the University of South Florida Special Collections Library. There are nearly one hundred boxes. Perhaps the answer lies therein. Someone will just need to find the time to go through them all.

And the stories do not stop there. There is also a young woman in a white dress who floats down the stairway wearing red high heels. And the ghost of a young boy playing ball has been both seen and heard at different times in the corridors. The Cuban Club has definitely earned its reputation as the most haunted place in Ybor City.

Chapter 6
SHOPS AND RESTAURANTS

The streets of today's Ybor City are crowded with shops offering everything from the mundane to the exotic, restaurants from the basic to exquisite cuisine and clubs offering alcohol, music and dancing for any taste. But when the town first got started in the late 1880s, there were only the factories and the tobacco workers' houses. Getting the goods and services that were the basic necessities of life was often difficult.

Ybor City's first answer to the problem was street vendors. Peddlers with pushcarts or makeshift stands sold milk, eggs and vegetables (often grown in their own gardens). A few sold other luxuries like pots and pans and sewing supplies. Clearly, more variety and convenience was needed. Many of these original street merchants saved their pennies until they had enough to open a store. Some of the Anglo-Americans from Tampa saw the opportunity and began businesses to provide goods and services to Ybor City.

By the dawn of the twentieth century, you could find nearly anything you needed to buy within the boarders of Ybor City. A group of Jewish merchants arrived from New Orleans and built storefronts in the New Orleans style, with overhanging balconies and residences over the shops. James Tokely, the poet laureate of Tampa, tells of how some of the shop owners would open up to a good friend or customer even after business hours were over. All you had to do was stand underneath the balcony and holler up to the merchant. If your emergency was dire enough—say you forgot to get your wife a present for her birthday—he would come down and open the shop for you to make your important purchase.

A café with a Panadería la Joven Francesca delivery van parked in front. *Courtesy Tampa-Hillsborough Public Library System.*

Home delivery also began. A milkman delivered daily bottles of fresh milk. An iceman would bring the ice for the icebox. You hung a sign out on your porch to let him know how much ice you needed. These signs listed four options. You hung the sign with the amount you wanted in the topmost position. Twenty-five pounds was enough for a couple or a small family. Larger families need fifty pounds. Seventy-five pounds meant you had company. And you only asked for one hundred pounds if there had been a death in the family.

Local bakeries would deliver fresh bread in unwrapped loaves. Each *casita* had a large nail on an outside wall near the door. The bakery's delivery boy would simply stick the loaf on the nail when he made his early morning rounds. When you got up, you just stepped out your front door, got your bread off the nail, brushed the bugs off and had your breakfast.

Seventh Avenue, also known as La Séptima, is still lined with the old buildings from the period. And some of the old inhabitants make their presence felt in the new establishments that occupy the space. Most of their stories are short and do not include an explanation for the haunting, but no account of Ybor City would be complete without these tales.

CARMINE'S

One restaurant that has become a fixture in Ybor City is Carmine's. Famous for its Spanish, Italian and Cuban cuisine, the restaurant offers a "front row window view of 7th Avenue," according to its website. On occasion, someone on the first floor will hear footsteps coming from the second floor. Upon investigation, there is no one to be found who could have made the footsteps. One waitress said she thought the building used to be a hospital, which might account for restless spirits, but this is unlikely. The building that houses Carmine's was always part of the commercial district along Seventh Avenue. The same waitress also said that she didn't like to go up to the second floor, as it left her with a very uneasy feeling. Perhaps this is appropriate for a restaurant that features a dish called "devil crabs"—deep fried croquettes

Balcony-level view along of Seventh Avenue. *Courtesy Tampa-Hillsborough Public Library System.*

of crabmeat and spices usually eaten with hot sauce. Carmine's, which is consistently listed as one of the best places to get this delicacy, has served the same recipe since around 1929. Could the ghostly footsteps just be the spirit of folks who want one last devil crab before going on to their final reward?

GASPAR'S GROTTO

Just across the street from Carmine's is Gaspar's Grotto. "It's a pirate bar," says Savannah, one of the managers. And that may be an understatement. The name is that of Tampa's legendary, albeit fictional, pirate, José Gaspar, who is the inspiration for a major festival every year. The bar's website claims it is a "one-stop bar hop." It offers food, live music, libations and special events—and perhaps a ghost or two. Eric, the owner, is more than willing to talk about the spirits, give you a tour of the bar and even show you photographic evidence.

This evidence is two pictures taken in 2004. There is a young boy posing in those pictures, but you can barely see him due to all the misty faces that appear around him (the ultimate ghostly photobomb). Some might suggest that this is just dust in the air or a defective camera. But those who work at Gaspar's remain convinced that several friendly ghosts continue to patronize the bar.

KING CORONA CIGARS

Its website says it is "the oasis of historic Ybor City," and that's probably right. Anytime it is open, from early morning to late at night, you will find King Corona Cigars brimming with people enjoying the ambiance. The place has fine cigars, fine wine, imported beers and delicious food. Its Cuban coffee is not to be missed, especially the café con leche.

Don and Brenda Barco are the owners. Brenda comes from a long line of Yborians. Her great-grandfather came from Cuba to roll cigars in the factories. Her grandfather started his own small factory, and the family has been connected to cigars and Ybor City ever since, through good times and bad. She and Don opened their shop in 1998. According to *Cigar Aficionado* magazine, King Corona is "one part cigar shop, one part cigar lounge, and one part bar." It also seems to be home to more than one ghostly resident. In fact, it advertises the Official Ybor City Ghost Tour on its website.

Back in 1998, two friends of the Barcos' were helping them with getting the building ready to open. One of these friends, Joe, was working late one evening installing some display cases when he felt a strong presence behind him. Turning, he saw a very large man standing in what is now the back hallway of the store. The vision seemed so real that Joe was getting ready to defend himself with his hammer against an attack, when the figure simply vanished. Another friend, Sarah, saw a young girl in a long dress from a bygone era. She called to the girl. But the figure simply faded away without giving any other response.

Who are these spirits? Like many of the specters of Ybor City, we cannot say for sure. But the history of the building may cast some light on the matter. For about sixty years, the building housed the dress shop of a man named Raul Vega. After that, it was an "upscale" women's store, La Nica Fashions, which is still in business but at a different location. After that closed, the building had been empty for two years before Don and Brenda began to work on it.

Could the male figure be the spirit of the merchant who ran a shop here for so many years? Could the young girl have been a member of his family or a customer? We will probably never know. However, it is interesting that, according to David Lapham's book *Ghosthunting Florida*, two different sensitives who visited the King Corona ten years apart came up with the same findings, each without knowing the history of the building or having the chance to compare notes with the other. The both felt the presence of blood in the back hallway where the male figure appeared. And they both felt the presence of a very sad young girl in the storeroom.

Whatever the explanation, no harm has ever come to anyone from these two spirits. A visit to King Corona is a definite must in Ybor City.

LA FRANCE AND REVOLVE

There are two shops on Seventh Avenue that may have the same ghost traveling back and forth between them.

The building at 1612 is a two-story structure, typical of those built by merchants in 1908. It is known as the B.F. Marcos Building, named after its original owner, Baldomero F. Marcos. The architect was Francis J. Kennard.

Like many of these buildings, it started off as shops on the ground floor with a residence above. Over the years, the space has been occupied by the Bank of Ybor City and the D'Elia Jewelry Store. But for thirty-nine years, it was the La France Shoe Store, run by two daughters of the original owner. The Marcos sisters were a fixture on Seventh Avenue from 1932 to 1973. The building even still has "La France" in tiles in the entryway. So it made sense for Jill Wax, the current shopkeeper, to take on the old name and call her store La France as well. Her shop has also been on this spot for nearly thirty years. It is not a shoe store, but you can buy shoes there, among other things. It is a very fine vintage clothing shop, featuring items for both men and women. You can also purchase new clothing there that looks like clothing from the past. About 25 percent of their inventory is "reproducible" clothing. Do you fancy an early twentieth-century tea dress or a beaded flapper dress from the 1920s? La France is definitely the place.

Seventh Avenue, looking west, with a view of automobiles, trolley and commercial buildings. *Courtesy Tampa-Hillsborough Public Library System.*

A few doors down is another intriguing clothing shop. Revolve Clothing Exchange describes themselves as an "innovative twist on regular old retail" because they "buy, sell and swap" both "new and experienced clothing."

Both shops report similar ghostly phenomena. When employees arrive in the morning and the shop has been completely empty overnight, they find clothing moved around, sometimes removed from hangers and dumped on the floor. Some workers at Revolve say they have seen a small boy darting between the clothing racks. Current employees Phelicia and Lindsay have never seen the lad, but they have seen the clothing items on the floor or moved about. And they agree that the store is haunted.

Is this a mischievous spirit who visits both stores after hours? Someone from long ago who wants to try on the vintage clothing and is not too careful about replacing things on the hangers? Or is it two or more different spirits? Could the activity at La France be the work of the Marcos sisters who ran the La France Shoe Shop for so many years?

There is also a theory that spirits can attach themselves to objects as well as locations. Perhaps different spirits come and go with the various vintage items stocked by La France and Revolve.

ISLAND FLOWERS

Just a few doors farther down is Island Flowers. The floral arrangements the shop makes for weddings, funerals and special events are truly unique and stunning. Its employees believe their ghost is a man caught in an indelicate situation. Back in 1920, long before Island Flowers occupied the space, the buildings behind it, which fronted on Eighth Avenue, were involved in some of the criminal enterprises in Ybor City—namely, gambling and prostitution. One evening, a fire swept through those buildings. Although, the structure that is now home to Island Flowers was not damaged, old scars from flame and smoke can still be seen on the back of the building.

Fires were a constant danger in the early years of Ybor City. Most of the early buildings were made of wood, and even the stately red brick factories contained a lot of wood in their construction as well as wooden furniture and fixtures. Florida's hot climate exacerbated the danger. But perhaps the biggest single threat of fire came from the fact that this was cigar city. Most men who lived in Ybor smoked three to seven cigars a day. Of course, these cigars needed to be lit (and often relit) with a

El Witt Cigar Co. truck in front of the public library. *Courtesy Tampa-Hillsborough Public Library System.*

match. A carelessly tossed match or an improperly extinguished cigar butt often led to fires.

Two different gentlemen at Island Flowers, Mario and Toby, have experienced the presence of a man. Mario said that he believes this to be a customer who was caught in the fire in the brothel in 1920 and perished. His shadowy figure has been seen coming into the shop, hurrying right through the closed back door. Mario believes he is still looking for a means of escape from that long-ago fire. Toby says that the spirit also plays with the front door of the shop. Like many retail establishments, the flower shop has an electronic bell that rings when the entrance door opens or closes. When there is just one or two people in the store, Tony says, the front door will swing back and forth several times, moved by unseen hands, making the bell ring several times in rapid succession. And, although it can be downright annoying, Tony still believes that their spirit is just playful and means no harm to anyone. "It is not a bad ghost," he says.

THE COLUMBIA RESTAURANT

No discussion of restaurants in Ybor City would be complete without a mention of the Columbia Restaurant, which is Florida's oldest restaurant and the oldest Spanish restaurant in the United States. Casimiro Henandez Sr., a Cuban of Spanish descent, came to Ybor City along with his family in 1902. He founded the Columbia in 1905, and five generations of descendants have continued to operate it to this day. The name comes from the patriotic song honoring the United States, "Columbia, the Gem of the Ocean." Over the years, it has grown from a small establishment to covering a full city block in its Ybor City location and now has several other locations throughout Florida.

This original location, at 2117–2127 Seventh Avenue, is well worth a visit for the ambiance as well as the food. There are eleven dining rooms, each with its own unique décor. There are interesting reproductions scattered among genuine museum-quality antiques, including a seventeenth-century

Columbia Restaurant Dining Room, as seen from the balcony level. *Courtesy Tampa-Hillsborough Public Library System.*

THE CUBAN SANDWICH

One of the most-ordered items for lunch at the Columbia is a "mixto," or Cuban sandwich. The traditional sandwich is a stack of Spanish ham, Cuban pork, swiss cheese, mustard and pickles, pressed on Cuban bread. When you get a Cuban in Ybor City, there is also salami. Many think this is in tribute to the fact that so many in the community are Italian. So the sandwich is like Ybor City itself, a melding of the flavors of Cuba, Spain and Italy, with a few extras from other cultures. Back in 2010, Richard Gonzmart, one of the owners of the Columbia, began to feel that he had not lived up to the legacy of past generations. The restaurant's Cuban sandwich was just not what it used to be. He set out to find out exactly why. He discovered that the modern processing of foods was the problem. They no longer roasted their own port or ham. It arrived premarinated and ready to slice. The meats were less moist and more salty than when they did it themselves. They were using a different kind of salami. Mr. Gonzmart realized that "over the years, short cuts had been taken." He decided to re-create the original sandwich. He started by getting his bread from La Segunda Bakery right in Ybor City—the same bakery that had supplied bread to the Columbia in his grandfather's day. They began roasting their own meat on the premises. The ham was given a sweetness from a sugary rub that caramelize on the edges. The pork was marinated overnight in a special sauce before it was roasted. He also discovered that everything had to be stacked in the exact right order, so that the juices from the salami and the tang of the mustard flowed in just the right manner.

Mr. Gonzmart is now happy with the Cuban sandwich at the Columbia. It was a lot of effort. And it does cost a bit more, but not that much. It is worth it to him and to the customers, as well, to once again offer the legendary Cuban of his grandfather's day.

tapestry, a 1935 vintage chandelier and an Asian vase. The latter may well have a value in the six-figure range. It is an intriguing and eclectic mix.

However, it does not have the reputation of being haunted. One server, who asked not to be identified, did say that sometimes there are unexplained happenings—simple things, nothing major. Ceiling fans will turn on and off for no apparent reason and without anyone touching the switches. Chairs have moved by themselves, as if being pulled away from the table by an invisible waiter to assist an invisible customer to her seat.

Perhaps this is the ghost of the most famous waiter of the Columbia. Some have even called him the most famous waiter in Tampa history. His name was Gregorio Martínez. He began working at the Columbia back in the days of Prohibition. According to official Columbia Restaurant history, Gregorio was working at a speakeasy nearby when the place was raided by federal authorities. Hoping to avoid arrest, Gregorio ran into the Columbia, pursued by the federal agents. As he was already wearing a tuxedo, he picked up a waiter's towel, threw it over his arm and proceeded to wait on tables at the Columbia, as if he were an employee. Once he had blended in this way, the agents were unable to identify him as their quarry and left. Gregorio just kept right on working at the Columbia and never went back to the speakeasy.

Mr. Hernández didn't care how Gregorio got the job; he just cared that he was an excellent waiter. It was said that Gregario never used a tray to deliver food and that he could carry as many as ten salad plates stacked up along his arms without ever breaking a dish. He did keep a pad of paper and wrote down his customer's orders. But what he may have lacked in memory, he certainly made up for in style.

He was a handsome man with dark, wavy hair and a large, luxurious mustache. People said he looked like the king of Spain, Alfonso XIII. So they called him *el rey*, or "the king"—a fitting title for the king of waiters. He stayed at the Columbia for many, many years. In the 1940s, he switched from evenings to the lunch shift because the bright lights at night hurt his eyes. Eventually, he retired. He died on October 23, 1976, and was buried in the Spanish Club Cemetery.

Could it be he returns to visit the old restaurant to this day? After all, he worked there for so many years he was almost part of the family. Is he just adjusting the ceiling fans for the comfort of the patrons and pulling out chairs for a lady who has come in for lunch?

Several famous people have visited the Columbia over the years, from old-time athletes like Babe Ruth to athletes of today like Derek Jeter. Liberace, Bruce Springsteen, Marilyn Monroe and Liza Minnelli have all

Right: Colonel Theodore Roosevelt on horseback in the Port of Tampa Florida. *Courtesy Tampa-Hillsborough Public Library System.*

Below: Columbia Restaurant at the corner of Seventh Avenue and Twenty-second Street in the early 1930s. *Courtesy Tampa-Hillsborough Public Library System.*

stopped by for lunch or dinner. The actor Jimmy Stewart visited here in 1954 while filming *Strategic Air Command*, and Robert Wagner came in 1953 during the filming of *Twelve Mile Reef*. So you will be in good company if you stop by for a 1905 salad (made table side), a pitcher of sangria, some Cuban bread and paella. You will be glad you did.

On another note, before the Columbia was built, back in the days of the Spanish-American War, there was a horse trough on this spot. Teddy Roosevelt and his Rough Riders would come here to water their horses. A plaque at the sight reads, "Colonel 'Teddy' Roosevelt frequently rode by here on his horse 'Texas' followed by his little dog, 'Cuba.'" There are those who still report to this day that they hear the sounds of men and horses and a dog barking near the site where the old water trough once sat.

Chapter 7

OTHER YBOR CITY BUILDINGS

DON VICENTE INN

This quaint boutique hotel looks as if it is very old. In fact it was only recently turned into a bed-and-breakfast inn after a fire that basically destroyed the original interior. Located at 1915 Fourteenth Street (also known as Avenida República de Cuba), it was built in 1895 to be the home of the Ybor Land and Improvement Company. It was here that Gavino Gutiérrez laid out the street grid for Ybor City and made plans for the city's amenities and architecture.

Gutiérrez was personally selected for this task by Mr. Ybor. He had faith in his abilities as a civil engineer, though some have suggested that Gutiérrez had highly embellished his credentials in that field. Whatever his background and skills upon his arrival here at the age of thirty-six, he proved capable of the task before him. He brought his family to Ybor and established his own fortune by buying 149 acres of land in the area, dividing it into parcels and selling the lots. He built his own home and named it Spanish Park. He died on a visit to Spain in 1919, and his body was not returned to Tampa until 1924. He is buried in Myrtle Hill Cemetery. His obituary acknowledges him as one of the founders of the cigar industry in Tampa.

Dr. José Ramón Avellanal, who helped with the founding of *La Gaceta* newspaper, was a great physician and humanitarian. Born in Spain and educated in Cuba, he founded a clinic in this building in the early twentieth century. He called it *El Bien Público*, or "the Public Good." By the time of Dr. Avellanal's death in 1927, the clinic had over twenty thousand members. There are still many Yborians today who will proudly tell you they were born in that clinic.

The clinic continued to operate after the good doctor's death, and in 1935, it was renamed the A.A. Gonzalez Clinic. That operated until 1968. After that, the building sat empty for decades. It was in 1998 that Jack Shiver bought the building with the intention of turning it into an inn. It was not to be an easy task. Jack said that in those early days, he could stand in the basement, look up and see the sky through the holes in the roof.

Jack decided to name the inn Don Vicente de Ybor to honor the city's founder. And it was important for him to make it look as though it had been an inn since it was first built in 1895. To that end, he and his daughter Tessa decorated the Don Vicente with antiques and reproductions. The sixteen rooms are meant to give you a glimpse into the early days of Ybor City. But you may also get a glimpse of something else from the past. Spirits from the days when this was a medical clinic might also be lingering. There are flickering lights, faucets that turn on and off by themselves and unexplained footsteps.

There is an apparition of a nurse that has been seen both in the basement area, which was the morgue for the clinic, and upstairs in some of the rooms. Sometimes she appears as young and lovely, and other times she appears as an old hag. Is this two different spirits, or one spirit that started young and aged during its service at the old clinic?

The most haunted room in the inn is room 305. Supposedly there was a murder/suicide that occurred on this spot. The room has frequent problems. Electric lights either refuse to work at all or turn on by themselves. The key card reader in the door often will not work, and the television malfunctions so often that guests complain about it.

Both Tessa and Jack say they have clearly seen a Spanish woman dressed in old-fashioned clothes. Tessa described her experience to the Travel Channel when the inn was featured on the *Dead Files* program in an episode called "Hotel Hell." She said, "I walked into the bathroom, turned on the lights and there she was. It was a ghost. I know that it was a Spanish woman. You could see right through her. She had no color." On that same episode, the *Dead File*'s medium said she also sensed a former nurse.

It would seem that just the fact that this was a former clinic with countless births and deaths over the years would be enough to explain these hauntings. But a persistent legend has grown up regarding Dr. José Ramón Avellanal's

The Don Vicente de Ybor Inn. *Author's collection.*

son, José Luis Avellanal. It has been published in ghost hunting guides, on websites and in YouTube videos that the younger José was a schizophrenic who conducted diabolical experiments on patients at the clinic, causing their deaths and then disposing of their bodies in the basement incinerator. When his gruesome activities were discovered, he was banned from the clinic and moved into an apartment in the El Pasaje across the street, where he continued to experiment on the prostitutes who worked in the brothel there. If they died, he would drag their bodies through a tunnel under the street to the basement of the clinic and once again make use of the morgue's incinerator. Really good, creepy story, right? However, it is total nonsense.

José Luis Avellanal was a respected member of the community. Yes, he was eccentric. As a boy, he built his own version of an electric chair and convinced one of his friends to try it out. Fortunately, it did not work. Yes, he did claim to be a doctor, though it is uncertain that he ever went to medical school. He did conduct odd experiments but not on people. He was an early advocate of cryogenics—that is, freezing the body so it can be revived later when there is a new cure for whatever caused death. But his experiments were on cats, not humans. He surely was a terror to the stray cats of Ybor City. And he used a lot of electricity in his unsuccessful attempts to revive them.

Yes, he did live at the El Pasaje but by choice, not because he was exiled there. In fact, eventually he came to own the El Pasaje after inheriting it from his mother, who had purchased it in 1945. He would sell diplomas from his bedroom, which he had gotten chartered as Southern University. He ran for the Florida State Senate and held services as an ordained Baptist minister. While on a visit to Cuba, he helped to found the Legion of Honor of the Republic of Cuba. When you joined the legion (there were really no qualifications necessary to do so), you got a certificate of honor and a medal. Soon, he was selling those from his bedroom as well. Then he packed up a box of the medals and headed for Mexico, hoping to sell them there. When he came back to Ybor City he was wearing the uniform of a general in the Mexican army, although it was not clear just how he had achieved that rank. He insisted ever after that he be addressed as "General" and once refused to grant an interview to one of Tampa's eminent local historians because he did not address him in that manner.

In the 1970s, he spearheaded a drive to save the El Pasaje from destruction. He is a big reason that the beautiful building still stands today. He finally passed away in 1982 at the age of ninety-six. If he really had been a mass murderer, surely he would have been found out and arrested long before that. His personal papers as well as those of his father reside in the Special Collections section of the University of South Florida Library.

So, no, he is not the reason for the ghosts at the Don Vicente, which makes perfect sense, for, as Tessa says, all their ghosts are good spirits. The name "Hotel Hell" turns out to be unjustified hyperbole. So stop by the inn, and Jack and Tessa will be happy you to introduce to their friendly ghosts. Or better yet, book a room in the old *El Bien Pública*. Room 305 is particularly nice—that is, if you don't want to watch television.

EL PASAJE

The building that covers nearly a city block at 1318 to 1330 Ninth Avenue draws the eye immediately for its beauty. Originally called "El Pasaje" for its open-air passageway along the outside, it was the second brick building constructed in Ybor City (the first was Mr. Ybor's factory). Money for the structure was donated by Mr. Ybor himself, and construction took place during 1886–88. The architectural style is "Eclectic with Italian Renaissance elements."

Purely commercial complexes are rare in Ybor City because most shop owners wanted to combine their business enterprise with their living space above the shop. The El Pasaje was built specifically to be an office building for Vicente Martínez de Ybor's many business interests. It was conveniently located across from his cigar factory complex. There were also sleeping rooms on the second floor. Each of these rooms had a leaded-glass transom in the window, which remain in place to this day. On careful observation, it is clear that each one of these transoms is different from the others—quite an artistic statement. At the time, Tampa had only one really good hotel, Henry Plant's Tampa Bay Hotel, which was quite a distance from the factories of Ybor City, so deluxe accommodations at the El Pasaje were much in demand. José Martí slept in this building on November 25, 1892.

The building took on a new use when it became the Cherokee Club, which opened on March 25, 1896. This was the most exclusive gentlemen's

A party on the colonnade of the Cherokee Club at the El Pasaje. *Courtesy of Ybor City State Museum.*

club in Tampa. Its membership was a unique combination of persons of both Latin and American heritage, but all were men of wealth and position. These important men would gather at the Cherokee Club for socializing, entertainment, gambling and general relaxation. The sleeping rooms continued to be available for members and out-of-town guests. Legend has it that there were also "ladies of the evening" who lived in some of those rooms, and they were available for hire.

There were several famous guests over the years, including Theodore Roosevelt and Frederic Remington. It was certainly one of Charlie Wall's favorite places. A plaque in front of the El Pasaje today claims that Winston Churchill once stayed there. However, Ybor City historian Gary Mormino claims that the plaque is in error and that Churchill never stayed there.

One frequent guest over the years was Edward Manrara, one of Ybor's partners. His wife hated the Florida climate, so she preferred to stay at their home in New York City. Therefore, although he owned a home on Ninth Avenue, when he traveled alone, he preferred to stay at the Cherokee Club. Despite the fact that his name is mostly unknown to today's visitors to Ybor City, he was an extremely important man in its development. In fact, the *Tampa Tribune* said of him in 1886: "Mr. Manrara is one of the most industrious and energetic men we have ever met. He speaks and writes English correctly and with ease. He is a good communicator, organizer, aside [from being] courteous and friendly. He displays the qualities of the true gentlemen, both in business and social intercourse."

Mr. Manrara was an essential help to Mr. Ybor, as the latter's command of English was limited. Also, Manrara was very astute financially, as he had worked in banking as a young man in Spain. When Ybor died, he left Manrara as sole proprietor of the Príncipe de Gales factory. He also was co-founder of the Florida Brewing Company and brought the first "horseless carriage" to Tampa in 1901. It is said that when the locals saw him coming in his automobile, they would cry out a warning to get out of the way, yelling, "Here comes the devil wagon!"

He was very distinctive in appearance. Although there was little hair left on his head, he made up for that lack with an abundance of facial hair. He had large, dark bushy eyebrows and a very large mustache that was carefully waxed to come up to perfectly pointed ends, well up on his cheeks.

Manrara passed away in New York City, surrounded by his family, on May 2, 1912. And despite his major contribution to the development of Ybor City, he was largely forgotten in Florida. And perhaps that forgetfulness on the part of Ybor City does not sit well with him in the afterlife. It has been reported that if one watches the second-floor windows at the El Pasaje in the early evening hours, you can see a misty face peering out at you. Although the features are indistinct, a bald head, bushy eyebrows and enormous waxed mustache can clearly be seen. And sometimes on a quiet afternoon, one can hear the sounds of an early automobile puffing its way down Ninth Avenue. Edward Manrara has been described as "the man forgotten by history." Perhaps he just wants to be remembered.

Time moved on. In 1924, a gentleman named José Álvarez bought the club and operated it as a restaurant called the El Pasaje. Although the club was technically closed during Prohibition, the restaurant and bar were the site of many private events and luxurious banquets. It is likely that illegal liquor flowed freely. In 1934, Álverez declared bankruptcy and sold the building in 1937 to Jefferson Standard Life Insurance Company, which in turn sold it, in 1943, to the Federation of Pan Am American Club, an organization dedicated to the promotion of the relationship and understanding between

Cigar manufacturers playing cards at the Cherokee Club. *Courtesy Tampa-Hillsborough Public Library System.*

the United States and Latin America. After only two years, the federation sold the property to Concepción Avellanal, the wife of Dr. José Ramón Avellanal, who founded the *El Bien Público*. She, in turn, willed the property to her son, José Luis Avellanal, who, as we have seen, was not a mass murderer. He owned the property until his death in 1982. His figure has also been seen walking along the open-air colonnade of the El Pasaje. He appears as an elderly gentleman wearing the uniform of a Mexican general. Perhaps he is haunting the area in hopes of dispelling the persistent myths that surround his life in Ybor City.

The El Pasaje has had many tenants over the past several years. In the early 2000s, the building was home to a lesbian nightclub, an alternative newspaper called the *Weekly Planet* and a popular Cuban restaurant called the Café Creole, which closed in the middle of that decade. The fading sign for the Café Creole is still hanging from the corner of the building. Today, the building is mostly empty, although there is neither a "for sale" nor a "for lease" sign. Its only visible tenant is the Radiant Group, a gas and oil corporation formed during the 1930s, which occupies suite 211. In the old nightclub space, dust gathers and silence reigns. How many spirits walk those empty halls and abandoned guest rooms? We will probably never know.

YBOR CITY STATE MUSEUM

Several different buildings make up the Ybor City State Museum on Ninth Avenue. From 1800 to 1804 are three *casitas*, or cigar workers' homes. These were originally built at other locations and moved here in 1976 and restored. When you visit the museum, be sure to ask the attendant to let you see the interior. It will give you an excellent idea of how the *tobaqueros* and their families lived.

The main building for the museum is an old bakery. In 1896, Francisco Ferlita (an Italian) opened a bakery on this spot in a wood-frame building. He called it La Joven Francesca Bakery. He got the name from a popular bakery in Cuba. He sold his bread for three to five cents a loaf. When the building burned to the ground in one of Ybor City's many fires, the ovens remained. Fire had no effect on the huge brick structures. So Mr. Ferlita simply built his new building around the old ovens. This time he used yellow brick in the construction to avoid future fires. When he reopened, he called it the Ferlita

Casitas are called "shotgun" houses because you could open the front door and the back door and fire a shotgun through the long hallway that connected the two. This design was used so that breezes could blow through and keep the houses cool. The rooms were usually few in number. There was a front porch. There would be a "front room," or sitting room, and usually two bedrooms, one for the parents and one for the children. Some homes were a bit bigger and may have had an additional room for other relatives who might be sharing the home, like the grandparents or a brother and his wife. Then there was a kitchen at the back.

Casitas were built on stilts to prevent flooding in the summer rains. And there were enough steps leading up to the front door so that alligators could not climb onto the porch. There was a place on the porch to hang the sign that showed the iceman how much ice you needed. And there was usually a large nail near the door so the bakery could impale your daily loaf of fresh bread when it was delivered early in the morning. Built from Florida pine, these homes had no heat, running water or electricity. They originally had roofs of cedar or cypress shakes, but after several fires ravaged the community, many of the wood roofs were replaced with tin.

There are very few of these homes left. Many were destroyed when I275 cut Ybor City in half. Many others have burned down or been torn down over the years. It is a rare look into the past to see these homes at the Ybor City State Museum.

Bakery. That is the building that still stands today. Francisco Ferlita died in 1931, but his five sons continued to run the business until 1973.

It is widely accepted that the first "Cuban bread" in the United States was baked at La Joven Francesca Bakery. Some of the characteristics of this type of bread developed from the need to feed large families in hard times. It is similar to French bread, but a small amount of lard is also added to the dough. It is baked in long loaves, much like a baguette but flatter. A damp palm frond is laid lengthwise on the loaf before it is baked, which gives the bread a distinctive groove down the center. The palm frond is removed as

The Queen Anne residence of John E. Ries, a German factory manager, was much grander than the casitas of the workers. *Courtesy Tampa-Hillsborough Public Library System.*

soon as the loaves leave the oven. Cuban bread is an essential ingredient in a traditional Cuban sandwich, which is now served all over Florida but has a strong connection to Ybor City.

The wood-frame building next door to the old brick bakery is now the museum gift shop. You can pick up a copy of *La Gaceta* or various other souvenirs. It also carries several books about the history of the area. It has been reported that a particular book in the gift shop had some odd habits. Copies of this book had been known to "jump off the shelves" or to move themselves to a different spot in the store, where they would be more prominently on display. The book was *Come to My Sunland: The Letters of Julia Daniels Moseley from the Florida Frontier, 1882–1886.* This was the same book that extolled the virtues of Dr. Frederick Weightnovel, one of the "bad guys" discussed earlier. Could it be Julia's spirit is still trying to come to the defense of her Russian friend? The gift shop no longer carries this book, as it is out of print, and there have been no further disturbances among the literature.

Two men standing near a railroad crossing with casitas in the backgrounds. *Courtesy Tampa-Hillsborough Public Library System.*

But within the old bakery building, there has been one other intriguing phenomenon. Early in the morning, when staff members are just opening up the museum, there is the smell of baking bread. Sometimes the smell is so strong that it is noticed out on the sidewalk or in the courtyard—a left over scent from the days of the La Ferlita Bakery?

Ritz

The corner of Seventh Avenue and Fifteenth Street is an important one in the history of Ybor City. It was here that another Cuban revolutionary held meetings in 1896. Most of men who strove for *Cuba Libre*, like José Martí, were either Spanish or Cuban born. But the man who made speeches here was actually Italian born. At the age of twenty, Orestes Ferrara was a young ℊ law in Naples, Italy. He became obsessed with the cause of ..eedom from Spain. He left a well-to-do family behind him and ..ed for Cuba. According to his contemporaries, he fought with as much ..ntensity as any native soldier.

He came to Ybor City, like José Martí, to raise funds and soldiers for the war of liberation. Eventually, he led a group of these Tampa followers on an expedition to Cuba. During this time, he had the reputation of being a ruthless "mambi," or Cuban freedom fighter. It was said that he beheaded hundreds of Spanish soldiers with his machete. This was probably an exaggeration, but it is an indication of how popular he became with the Cuban people.

After the victory in the Spanish-American War, Ferrara returned to Italy to complete his law degree. But he returned to Cuba immediately after he became an attorney and established one of the finest law firms in Havana. He went on to serve in many important positions for the Republic of Cuba. In 1940, he survived an assassination attempt. Even after being hit by ten bullets, he calmly got into a taxi and went to the emergency room. He went on to serve as Cuban secretary of state, ambassador to the United States and delegate to UNESCO. There are many who believe that he would have become president of Cuba if he had been born in Cuba instead of Italy.

He lived long enough to see the death of his dream of a Cuban republic. After Castro took over, Ferrara moved back to Italy, where he made his home in Rome's Grand Hotel until his death in February 1972 at ninety-six.

There are those who say if you stand at the corner of Seventh Avenue and Fifteenth Street and listen very carefully, you can still hear the sounds of the cheering crowd, carried away by the fiery oratory of Orestes Ferrara.

Next to the spot where revolutionaries met stands the Ritz Ybor at 1503–1507 Seventh Avenue. At the time this building was constructed in 1917, Ybor City was an established area, still in its glory days. It began as the Rivoli Theatre, where you could see a live performance for fifteen to thirty-five cents. It is a red brick building, with offices/apartments on the second floor. It is true that nearly every older theater building has a ghost. Perhaps it is because so many people come and go. Or perhaps it is because so many fictional characters have been portrayed on stage or screen. But often a violent death can also bring on a haunting. And the Ritz is no exception.

The history of the Ritz is long and diverse. There have been live plays, silent films, nude dancers and rock concerts. In recent years, it has even been the site of private parties, corporate events and formal affairs. Over time it has been known as the Rivoli, the Ritz, the Manchester and the Masquerade, and it is now the Ritz again.

In the 1920s, people stood in line for tickets to see Rudolph Valentino, the great silent film matinee idol. In 1945, the building was expanded and became the Ritz for the first time. During the 1940s, this was the place were all the teens and young adults hung out. Many a marriage had its start with young people holding hands in the dark and stealing kisses in the back rows. In the 1960s and 1970s, it was still a movie theater but was heading steadily downhill. News stories were all about what an unsavory place it had become. In 1966, it was renamed the Ritz Adult Theatre. Movies shown were often very "blue." It was also during these years that live nude burlesque acts were added, featuring such beauties as "48-24-36 Queen of the College Campus" and "Minnie the Mermaid." Despite the bad press, the building was added to the National Register of Historic Places in 1973 and to the Ybor City Historic District in 1989.

In the late 1980s, there were about a dozen people living in rat-trap apartments above the old theater. They protested being evicted by the Freedom Savings and Loan when the bank foreclosed on the property, saying they were never given any notice until officials showed up to start changing the locks. Legend says that a young lad who lived in the apartments during the 1920s was playing with a rope on the balcony that jutted out over the street. Somehow, he accidentally hanged himself. To this day, the anguished cries of his mother can be heard coming from the second floor.

In 1988, the Capitano family, longtime Ybor City residents, purchased the property and gave it a new lease on life. After a brief closure for remodeling, the property was leased to a nightclub called the Masquerade. From that time until 2006, it was a successful rock band venue. However, the nightclub closed in 2006, owing the Capitano family over $90,000 in back rent.

At that time, the Capitanos decided to run it themselves as an event center. In 2013, they merged the Ritz with another club they owned across the street, the Czar (that building is currently empty, but the sign that says Czar can clearly be seen). And the Ritz Ybor is once again one of the hottest places in town for both concerts and private events.

But what about that violent death? It happened back in June 2005 at the Masquerade. The heavy metal band Corrosion of Conformity was playing to a relatively small crowd of about 250 people. A couple young women, Wendy Laskas and a friend, who was never identified in the newspaper accounts (most likely because she was a minor), inadvertently knocked over a young man in the mosh pit. At first, there didn't appear to be a real problem;

the young man, whose name was Michael Pyne, got up, brushed himself off and shook the ladies' hands. "It's all good," he said. Then, noticing that both of the women sported tattoos, he mentioned that he was a tattoo artist and gave them a business card from the Rat-a-Tac-Tat tattoo parlor in nearby Dunedin. No harm, no foul.

However, Michael's girlfriend seemed to be much more offended than Michael himself, and later on in the bar, she ran up to Wendy Laskas and her friend and began yelling at them. Wendy's husband, Thomas Laskas, jumped to the defense of his wife and her friend. Michael Pyne then entered into the fracas. It appeared that he was using his fists in the way one would normally use a knife. He started in on Thomas and then turned to Wendy and a man named Nicholas Stegall (apparently he was the boyfriend of the unidentified woman). Then Michael ran out the door. Things seemed quite unclear in the dark bar, but as Thomas Laskas stumbled toward the lighted hallway it became clear that Michael Pyne actually had had a knife in his fist. "There was blood everywhere," said one witness. Four people had been stabbed. A bartender had minor injuries and was treated at the scene. Nicholas Stegall had a puncture wound in his stomach, but was treated at the hospital emergency room and then released. Wendy Laskas was admitted to the hospital for her wounds, but her condition was never worse than "fair." But her husband, Thomas, had been stabbed multiple times, and he died from his wounds.

No one seemed able to identify the assailant. But police had the business card from the tattoo parlor. What they discovered was that Michael Pyne was the only employee in that establishment other than the owner. He was apprehended with the help of Russell Ramsey, his employer. At the end of the trial just over a year later, he was sentenced to twenty-five years in prison for the murder.

But often, a trial and a sentence bring neither peace nor closure. It has been reported that bloodstains are still on the floor near where the stabbings occurred, and they resist all efforts to clean them up. It has also been said that there seems to be a very helpful ghost that attends concerts at the Ritz Ybor to this day. When a patron trips or is bumped and is in danger of falling, they often feel a steadying hand grabbing their arm to keep them upright or perhaps pressing against their back to keep them safe. Is this the spirit of Thomas Laskas, wanting to prevent another tragedy like the one that happened to him on that hot June night in 2005?

Chapter 8

WEST TAMPA

THE OTHER CIGAR CITY

Ybor City itself was not the only cigar city in the late nineteenth and early twentieth centuries. There was another town called West Tampa; it has been mentioned a few times earlier in this book, and it was its own city, not a section of Tampa itself. It maintained its status as an independent town for longer than Ybor City did.

Like Vicente Martínez de Ybor, the founder of West Tampa was a man with a vision. But he was neither a Cuban nor a Spaniard. He was born on December 28, 1851, though sources conflict over exactly where; it was either Scotland or England, so definitely a part of what we today call the United Kingdom. His name was Hugh C. McFarlane. His family moved to America when he was still quite young, and he was educated in Massachusetts and Minnesota. He went to Boston University Law School and began a law practice in Fall River, Massachusetts.

He married Miss Sarah Brown, and they had a son, James. Unhappy in his marriage and feeling a bit of wanderlust, McFarlane divorced his wife, dissolved his law practice and headed south. He lived in New Orleans for a short time, but the Big Easy apparently did not satisfy his needs. So he headed to the Gulf Coast of Florida and to Tampa just as it was starting to thrive again after the arrival of Plant's railroads. At first, he had no plans to enter the cigar trade but had decided to practice law. He represented several defendants in high-profile murder cases. He developed the reputation of being able to get jurors to empathize with the accused, and he won several unexpected acquittals. He became a member of the board of trade and city attorney for Tampa. But his ambitions ran stronger than that.

In 1892, inspired by what he saw happening in Ybor City, he decided to found a town of his own. To that end, he purchased two hundred acres of forested land in the hopes that cigar manufacturers would bring their businesses there. He paid $2,000 for the same parcel of land that had sold for a mere $120 less than six months before. Perhaps he overpaid, but nonetheless, his timing was perfect. With the growth of the cigar industry in Ybor City, he was convinced that his new town, which he christened "West Tampa," could rise in the same manner.

There was one small problem. The Hillsborough River was a barrier between his new town and the Cuban/Italian/Spanish workforce that was living in Ybor City. McFarlane solved that problem in 1893 by building the Fortune Street Bridge and then began the development of a public streetcar line to bring the workers to the halls of the new cigar factories in West Tampa. Then he made it known to cigar manufacturers in Key West that he was willing to construct buildings and donate land for factories if they would move their enterprises to West Tampa.

The first to take him up on his offer were the Del Pino brothers, who produced the first West Tampa cigar on July 15, 1892. However, their factory closed just one year later, citing problems getting workers and raw materials. The O'Halloran Cigar Co., also from Key West, had moved into the empty factory building by April 30, 1894. By that time, there was a ready labor force, as McFarlane, taking a page from Ybor's book, had built inexpensive employee housing, so that workers could be lured to his side of the river. By 1895, the population of West Tampa was 3,500 with 30 cigar factories. At its height there were 190 factories. West Tampa was incorporated as a city on May 18, 1895, and it was a separate town from Tampa proper for twenty-nine years.

In 1924, Hugh McFarlane was still an important force in West Tampa, and at that time, he and other city officials agreed that the time had come to become part of the larger city. He said, "We have transformed this swampland to a humming, buzzing and prosperous center for years to come. There have been two cities for thirty years, but always the intentions have been one. But over all we need to thank those cigar workers, because they made this possible. Thanks to the cigar industry."

At first, some of the residents resisted the merge. They complained about "the octopus" that was about to swallow them. But eventually they changed their minds and became loyal citizens of Tampa.

An electric streetcar full of passengers. *Courtesy Tampa-Hillsborough Public Library System.*

Annexation became official on January 1, 1925, and West Tampa ceased to exist as its own civil entity, but many of the factory buildings stand proudly to this day as the legacy of Hugh McFarlane.

McFarlane died in 1935, ten years after what he had built from the ground up became a proud part of the city of Tampa. And there are ghosts that linger in some of the old buildings and even in some of the new ones.

Santanella Cigar Factory

At 1906 North Armenia Avenue sits a cigar factory that was founded by a Spaniard and a German, an unusual combination for those days. Antonio Santanella was from Seville, Spain. His partner, Sol Hamburger (yes, really, that was his name), was from Bavaria. It turns out that this unlikely combination was very successful. It was said that Santanella was a genius at making cigars, and Hamburger was a genius at selling them. The two men opened a factory in Key West in 1886, moved their operation to West Tampa a few years later and remained successful throughout the Roaring Twenties and the Depression years. Even in 1946, when many other cigar companies were falling apart, Santanella Cigar Factory was still doing so well that it opened another factory in the area, across Tampa Bay in Clearwater. The company was sold in 1955 to the Universal Cigar Corporation, and this factory stayed in operation until 1989, when Universal Cigar moved all production to New Jersey. But the building still saw good use, as it was occupied by the Southern Millwork Co. When you walk by the building today, you can still see the words "Southern Millwork" in faint letters on the sides.

The building that stands today was built in 1904, after the two previous buildings on the spot had been destroyed by fire. Santanella and Hamburger were very clever with the designing of this latest factory. Since the previous two fires had started elsewhere and jumped from building to building, they reasoned they would be safer if their building was set apart. So they purchased the entire city block, locating their new factory in the middle, away from other buildings. Furthermore, they gave a parcel of their new block to the City of West Tampa to be used as a location for a fire station. That fire station remains to this day. It does help to have the fire station close by.

During the height of its business, Santanella Cigars made a fine "Clear Havana" cigar called the Óptimo. It was the top of their line, highly prized for its mild taste and commonly referred to as "the best of the best." There were several famous people who favored this cigar and would smoke this brand and no other. It was Winston Churchill's favorite. He purchased so many that one worker, a woman named Maria, always hand rolled his cigars just the way he liked them.

Another celebrity who preferred to smoke the Óptimo was Babe Ruth, the famous New York Yankee baseball player. He often paid visits to the Tampa Bay Area during March and April of each year during the 1930s, as Yankee spring training was held in nearby St. Petersburg. He would always make sure to visit the Santanella factory to personally purchase several boxes of this special cigar. He got to be good friends with the manager and assistant manager of the factory, and they would often play golf together.

The current owners of the building are students of the cigar making days in West Tampa and are dedicated to the preservation of the building and its history. The Ellis and Van Pelt families purchased the building in

1997 and began to operate Elis-Van Pelt Office Furniture Dealers from the old cigar factory. Since they did not need the entire building for their business, they converted the top two floors to artist studios, which have now been rented by a lot of local artists. They make use of the wide hallways, with their beautiful wooden floors, to display their art and offer art shows and exhibitions.

Mr. W. Grey Ellis has participated in a remarkable "mini-documentary" that can be found on YouTube. In it, he gives a full tour of the old factory building and talks about its lengthy history and about some of the souls who seem unable to leave the premises.

He points out the huge old safe, probably too big to ever be moved as long as the building stands. He explains that the reason for such a large safe was for the cigar makers' payroll. As most of them came from Cuba, they distrusted United States paper money. So it was determined that the best way to pay them was in silver dollars—obviously, a bulky method of payment. He also talks about how when the workers were paid at the end of the week, each one would leave one of his silver dollars under his rolling mat, as a kickback to the managers. If an employee failed to do this, he would most likely find himself, and all of his family, out of a job.

In his office, Mr. Ellis has a small museum of artifacts that he has found over the years in the nooks and crannies of the building's four stories that include cigar boxes, workers' tools and even some of the workers' chairs, handmade and upholstered on the seat and back with goatskin.

But it is when describing the ghosts in the building that he becomes the most animated. He obviously considers these spirits to be his friends. Two of the artists who came to work in the building over the years have passed away. Both of them, a man named Thomas and a man named Boris, have been seen walking through the halls of the art studio floors.

The spirits in the rest of the building are difficult to pin down. One of the women who works for Mr. Ellis is Angela. She describes coming into work early one morning and being in the building all by herself. As she sat working at her desk, she distinctly heard the door to the office open and footsteps across the creaky wooden floor. "Good morning," she called out to who she assumed was a co-worker. No response. Then she heard the door to the microwave in the break room open and close. "Good morning," she called again. Still no response. When she went to investigate, she found there was no one in the office, and the outer door was still securely closed and locked. She immediately left the building and waited outside until someone else living arrived to keep her company.

Gutiérrez Building on Northeast corner of Seventh Avenue and Sixteenth Street. *Courtesy Tampa-Hillsborough Public Library System.*

On another occasion, she and a colleague were working alone in the building late in the evening when the shadowy figure of a man appeared and moved right through the desk where they were sitting. And once again they heard those disembodied footsteps across the wooden floor. They did not hesitate. They locked up the office and went home.

Mr. and Mrs. Ellis were also interviewed for *Cigar City Magazine* in 2013. Although most of the interview concerned architecture and history, at the end they did discuss the possibility that the old factory was haunted. Mr. Ellis explained how an artist working late one night had a decorative sword hanging on the wall. Suddenly it began to turn slowly, and then it stopped as suddenly as it had started. Just who are these spirits? Again, we may never know for sure, but there certainly are intriguing possibilities: Babe Ruth come to look for his order of his favorite cigars? One of the factory owners who likes to return to make certain his legacy remains secure? After all, Sol Hamburger died quite young. He was only forty-nine years old when he succumbed to "paralysis of the heart." Or perhaps it is, as the interviewer speculated, one of the cigar workers who has just realized he forgot to leave a silver dollar under his rolling mat. And he is hurrying back into the factory to preserve his job and the jobs of his family.

HOPEWELL CHURCH CEMETERY

Near the busy corner of Dale Mabry and what is now known as Kennedy Boulevard in West Tampa, there are two cemeteries standing side by side. One belongs to the American Legion post, which is next door, whose members still maintain their graveyard. The other, surrounded on three sides by a red brick wall with a huge wrought-iron gate along the side facing Kennedy Boulevard, is the Hopewell Church Cemetery. Do not go looking for Hopewell Church, as it burned down more than a century ago, but the families who owned plots continue to care for the small burial site, and as their loved ones have passed from this world, their mortal remains have come to rest here. It is these same families who look after the cemetery to this day.

Many prominent early Tampans are buried here. And it is mostly a quiet place. But there have been disturbances in the past.

On May 27, 1983, the *Evening Independent* newspaper reported that the severed head of a goat and the cut off legs of chickens, with the feet and the feathers still attached, had been found in Hopewell Cemetery. The paper speculated that this was the work of a voodoo cult in West Tampa. Several years later, in July 2006, the *Tampa Tribune* reported a similar incident; this time, there was no goat's head, just a chicken with its throat slit, some candles and a doll tucked into a paper bag.

Although we think of voodoo as a New World religion, its origins actually go back to African beliefs in magic and sorcery. Brought here by enslaved persons from Africa, it changed to accommodate some parts of the Roman Catholic faith The particular brand of voodoo practiced in Cuba was call *brujería*.

The word *brujería*, which simply means witchcraft in Spanish, has come to signify the form of voodoo that was practiced in Cuba and that was, no doubt, brought to Tampa Bay by some of the Afro-Cuban cigar makers. At one time, both Ybor City and West Tampa had shops where one could buy the items for the casting of voodoo spells.

Were these strange items found in the cemetery part of some voodoo ritual? Let us be clear: there is no connection between those buried in the cemetery and voodoo. It is most likely that the people who left these items behind were just looking for a quiet and spooky place to practice their rituals. Some of their particular beliefs are that a person's possessions are an extension of the essence of that person, and by acting upon those possessions, you cause that person harm or happiness. They might have been using the doll as a means of a curse or a blessing. Practitioners of the faith see the world as a balance of good and evil and believe both must exist in harmony in order for the world to function.

The caretakers of Hopewell Church Cemetery have said that, just at dusk, they hear sounds coming from within the grounds. As they go in to investigate, the sounds get louder and more distinct, until clearly it is the sound of a woman crying out in grief and anguish. However, as they are closing in on the sound, everything suddenly falls silent. No living person has ever been found in the area when these sounds are heard. Is this just a mourner from one of the old Tampa families buried here? Perhaps she mourns for departed loved ones but does not yet know that she is dead herself. Or is this a spirit who is still trying to find her way to peace and rest after a brush with *brujería*? Those who follow the voodoo path will tell you that the worst thing that can happen to a person is to be turned into a zombie, to wander the earth forever without a soul. Let us hope that the painful cries of sorrow are not coming from such a being!

HOWARD W. BLAKE HIGH SCHOOL

Back in 1956, the year Howard W. Blake High School was established, public schools in Tampa and throughout Florida were still segregated. Named for a Tampa native son who made it his mission to help young people realize their full potential through education, it was one of only two high schools open to African American students during those days. It was in a different building than the one it occupies today. When Tampa schools were integrated in the 1960s, Blake was strictly a seventh-grade center. It remained so until 1997, when it opened in its new building and became a magnet school for the visual, communication, journalism and performing arts, including theater, music and dance. Those programs often win awards and honors for excellence, and the school carries an "A" rating from the State of Florida.

Apparently, it also carries a few spirits.

The place where the building now stands was once the site of the Clara Frye Negro Hospital. Clara was a trained nurse, born in Albany, New York, in 1872. She was the daughter of an African American man from the South and a white woman from England. She moved to Tampa in 1908. In those days, blacks and whites were not treated in the same facilities. When she found out from a local physician that an African American patient would die if he did not have surgery and there was no place willing to allow the operation, she offered her own home for the surgery. The patient survived. She eventually, with some help from the City of Tampa, opened her hospital in 1923. She never turned away anyone of any race from treatment, even if the person were unable to pay. She had a deep and abiding religious faith that moved her to help others. She died in 1936 at the age of sixty-four. She was all but destitute after pouring all her energy and all her money into care of the community. She was a great woman. Her hospital was closed in 1967 and torn down, but by then, Tampa General Hospital was fully integrated.

Students at Blake are convinced that spirits of some of the people who died in Clara Frye Hospital haunt the halls of their building. They believe that "B Building" was built over the site of the hospital's morgue. A drastic drop in temperature can be felt when walking down the corridors, even when the air conditioning is not working. The smell of antiseptics and other hospital smells are also prevalent, even when there is no possible source for the odor.

Cold spots in the auditorium are attributed to the death of a teacher who died of a heart attack during a pep rally. And sitting at the back tables in the library will cause hair to stand on end and chills to run up the spine. But the most haunted area at Blake seems to the theater. Strange lights are seen in the wings, and something seems to go wrong in every performance. Of course, that could just be the nature of live theater. But the students definitely believe.

Chapter 9

YBOR CITY TODAY

THE DEMISE OF THE CIGAR INDUSTRY

There have been many changes in Ybor City over the years. Like many boomtowns from the pioneer years in Florida, it has seen many ups and downs.

The 1920s were truly the greatest years for the cigar industry. With the blossoming new middle class all across the country, the demand for quality cigars increased. Assembly lines caused prices to fall on all manner of goods, including automobiles and other things that had once been out of reach for the average citizen. Some cigar factories began to toy with mechanization, but most continued to make their cigars as they always had, hand rolled by skilled, reasonably well-paid workers. There was no trouble getting the tobacco they needed from Cuba, and methods of shipment were improving, increasing the reach of their markets.

The downside to the 1920s was the rise of organized crime in Ybor City. This was the decade in which Charlie Wall truly became the "King of Tampa." Everyone played *bolita* from the bottom of society to the top. Charlie's operations continued to grow as he expanded into bootleg liquor, speakeasies and prostitution. Although smaller criminal groups tried to force their way in, Charlie Wall continued to hold all the cards. He openly bribed officials and bought voters and elections.

He may have been the biggest player in town, but he wasn't the only one. There was a small Italian gang led by Santo Trafficante Sr. In the 1930s, this rivalry would grow into a bloody war.

Aerial view of Ybor City, Florida Brewing Company. *Courtesy Tampa-Hillsborough Public Library System.*

Of course, the Roaring Twenties was also the decade of Prohibition in the United States. This amendment to the U.S. Constitution—along with its enforcing congressional mandate, the Volstead Act—prohibited the sale, manufacture, import or transport of alcoholic beverages anywhere within the country. Tampa, like most large cities was really not interested in enforcement, and alcohol consumption actually went up. In fact, all Prohibition did was make Tampa's already wide-open morals worse, corrupt law enforcement and encourage the growth of the criminal element.

But the cigar industry continued to thrive.

The 1930s began to change all of that. The stock market "crashed" in October 1929. Stock prices, which had been artificially inflated by speculation, dropped precipitously. Approximately $30 billion in stock values would disappear in less than a month. Many investors, both small and large, rushed to pull their savings out of banks before they could fail. Of course, that only made the bank failure inevitable.

The Citizens Bank and Trust Company of Tampa closed its doors. In fact almost all the banks in Ybor City either failed completely or teetered on the brink for years. Much like it would later happen in the early twenty-first century, what had once been expensive properties were suddenly worthless, but owners had mortgage obligations that still required substantial payments. Bankruptcies and foreclosures followed. Many businesses closed. Suicide rates went up. And there were very few people who could still afford a fine, hand-rolled cigar. Yes, people still wanted their tobacco, but it now was more often purchased in the form of cheap nickel cigars, chewing tobacco and cigarettes.

Since the factory owners had managed to defeat the workers in the strikes of 1920 and 1931, despite the workers' getting assistance from Charlie Wall, they felt free to start to mechanize operations to make cheaper cigars more quickly and profitably. Of course, this was not something they could do overnight. The cigar-making machines required significant capital investment, and those employees who were being retained needed to be trained to use the new machines. But little by little, the changes happened. A single cigar-making machine could do the work of twenty people rolling by hand. By the early years of the Depression, the reduction in demand and the mechanization of the process caused thousands of cigar workers to be laid off. Seventeen of the largest factories closed completely between 1929 and 1931. La Séptima began to look like a mere shadow of its former self. Ybor City had entered its decline.

The culture of Ybor City was dealt another serious blow by the Spanish civil war from 1936 to 1939. Those of both Cuban and Spanish descent fervently supported the Republic of Spain against General Franco. Many gave large portions of their salaries to the cause, and a few even went overseas to fight as part of the "Lincoln Brigade" that was formed in Tampa and fought in Spain in 1937. When Franco finally triumphed, many in Ybor City completely severed their ties to Spain.

And disaster struck again on Thursday, June 2, 1932, when the Cigar Manufacturers Association decreed that the position of *lector* was forever abolished. A way of life vanished when the sound of the radio replaced the cultured tones of the educated readers of Ybor City.

Organized crime increased its stranglehold as well in the 1930s and into the 1940s. There were more than a dozen killings of racketeers and at least six attempted assassinations in the two decades.

There was a bit of a renewed energy during World War II due to the large military presence in the Tampa Bay area. Airmen stationed at Macdill Army Airfield would come into Tampa for recreation. And the bars, restaurants and movie theaters of Ybor City were full of young men, eager to get a last taste of home before being sent overseas.

The end of World War II brought increased prosperity to many neighborhoods throughout the United States, particularly the new and rapidly growing suburbs. The prosperity did little for Ybor City. Although there was some renewed interest in fine cigars throughout the country, it was not enough to revive the industry. And what work was available was often now going to "crackers," or native Floridians, rather than the traditional Cubans, Spaniards and Italians. Many young men returning from the war found little reason to return to Ybor City and moved away.

Three serious blows fell on Ybor City in the 1960s. First, with Fidel Castro's ascent to power, an embargo was imposed on Cuba by the United States. There would be no more tobacco coming from Havana. What was left of an industry founded on the importation of Cuban tobacco reeled from the blow. As an interesting side note, President John F. Kennedy asked his press secretary, Pierre Salinger, to quietly obtain 1,200 Cuban cigars before the embargo went into effect. Reportedly, the president did get his cigars. So he was enjoying Cuban tobacco long after the rest of the country had started going without.

Second, an urban renewal program was supposed to build new projects in Ybor City. Many families and businesses were forced to move to make way for new buildings. But the funds dried up and the new buildings never materialized, leaving many empty lots behind. But the final deathblow was Interstate Highway 275, which cut right through the heart of Ybor City, destroying a large swath of the city and effectively cutting what remained in two.

Several interesting ideas were proposed for rehabilitating Ybor City during the late 1960s. One fascinating idea was to turn the whole area into a sort of Spanish "walled city" theme park, complete with "bloodless" bullfights. They did try to have an exhibition of this, but the bull escaped and ran amok in the streets, eventually having to be shot by a sheriff's deputy with a high-powered rifle. Needless to say, that idea was rejected.

TOURIST AND CLUB INDUSTRY

It was finally a new industry that began to turn things around for Ybor City once again. In the 1980s, young artists from various fields turned to

Ybor City for inexpensive housing and exhibition space. They helped to usher in a vibrant nightclub scene, which brought a great deal of people and money into Ybor City. However, it was not always the most desirable element who came to the clubs. And many longtime residents complained of the rowdiness, congestion and noise.

So since 2000, the city has put more emphasis on a more balanced use of the area. Tourists and families are encouraged to visit in addition to nighttime revelers. Although the club scene can still be a bit on the shady side and there is still violence at night from time to time, this does appear to be improving. During the day, Ybor City is a perfectly safe and family-friendly environment. Chickens and roosters freely roam the streets, a tourist attraction in and of themselves. There is a complex called Centro Ybor that includes a movie theater, restaurants and shops. In 2009, IKEA, the Swedish furniture manufacturer, opened up its largest store in Florida on the edge of Ybor City. Furthermore, many of the new attractions are tied to the old days. Several restaurants now feature both Cuban and Spanish cuisine. Café con leche, a strong Cuban coffee served with scalded milk, can be found nearly everywhere. Stop by King Corona Cigars for a cup. The Columbia Restaurant is more popular than ever. Despite its very large size, it can still be difficult to get a table there on the weekends. La France vintage clothing and Revolve continue to operate, offering unique attire and a friendly atmosphere. The Ybor City State Museum has much for you to see and do. The social clubs that are still functioning offer ethnic events open to the public. And best of all, as you walk down Seventh Avenue, there are some shops that have tables and chairs in the windows, and seated at that table is a man, or sometimes a woman, hand rolling a fine cigar. And although the tobacco does not come from Cuba, the Oliva Tobacco Company is still in business, and they grow tobacco in Nicaragua and Honduras from seeds of strains of tobacco brought from Cuba generations ago.

No, of course, Ybor City is not what it used to be. And it probably never will be. But it is a vibrant and lively section of Tampa that continues to celebrate its unique heritage.

GUAVAWEEN AND FANTASMA FEST

Perhaps there is no better illustration of what Ybor City has become and how it continues to evolve than the festival of Guavaween. It is fascinating that there is now a festival named for the fruit that Bernardino Gárgol and Gavino Gutiérrez did *not* find here in 1884. It seems that a newspaper columnist named Steve Otto, who wrote for the *Tampa Tribune* for forty-five years before retiring in July 2014, once quipped that if New York was the Big Apple, then Tampa must be the Big Guava. The nickname appealed so much to some people that they decided to make a festival out it. Guavaween, as the name might suggest, is held in the fall, usually just before Halloween.

It seems to have originated out of two separate events. One was an idea that started in the 1970s when the young artists were first moving into the area. They decided to have a Halloween party and charge everyone a single dollar to participate. At about the same time, another group started the "Artists and Writers Ball," which was originally held in late February as a sort of "underground alternative" to Gasparilla, which is Tampa's big pirate festival held at that time of year.

Eventually, these two events were merged together into one huge event that attracted thousands of people to Ybor City to celebrate. It was a little more raucous at its inception in 1985 that it is today. It started off as a sort of celebration of drinking and debauchery with revealing costumes, and Seventh Avenue was fenced off so that the whole area became a drinking zone. But it has evolved into a full-day event with a "Family Funfest" during the day with activities for children as well as adults. Scavenger hunts, food, rides, a children's costume contest and parade and, of course, safe trick-or-treating.

In the evening, things do take a more risqué turn, as Mama Guava takes center stage with her loyal band of followers. According to the Guavaween legend, Mama Guava is the child of the pirate José Gaspar by a scrub palmetto tree, which I'm sure is a biological impossibility. Mama says she is taking the "bore" out of Ybor. The celebration is the primary fundraiser for the Ybor City Chamber of Commerce.

But in 2014, the Ybor City Chamber is looking for someone else to run the festival. Attendance has been declining for years, and some of the merchants feel it isn't worth the effort. Others feel that popularity has been dropping only because things are not as wild as they used to be. But the festival is not in danger. If the chamber members cannot find a company to run it, they will run it again themselves.

There are some who think it should go back to its roots. Ilya Goldbert, who owns the Stone Soup Company on Seventh Avenue, believes that Guavaween started out as a party and it should stay that way. Merchants who don't like it should move their stores to a nice quiet suburb. "For years,

Guavaween worked as an adult-only event, a big party, and a good time. There's absolutely nothing wrong with that," he said. "It's one night. We wake up, we have a hangover, we clean up and move on." Perhaps that last statement is a good motto for Ybor City over all the years.

In 2012, Guavaween added a new festival within a festival called Fantasma Fest. Organizers claim that, since it is near Halloween, they are honoring one of Ybor City's many ghosts. And although the story they tell is almost certainly completely made up, it is a good story and seems a good way to end a book about haunted Ybor City.

The official ghost story of Fantasma Fest goes like this:

In 1902, a young man named César León was a cigar roller in an Ybor City factory. He was quite popular with his fellow workers, and he developed a special friendship with an older worker named Juan Prado, who took young César under his wing and helped him to become a more accomplished artisan. As time went on, César fell in love with his friend's daughter, Carmen, and wanted to marry her. But Juan would not consent.

Carmen had broken her leg badly as a child, and the leg had been poorly set and never healed properly, leaving her with a pronounced limp and the need of a cane. Her father felt that she would not want to walk down the aisle of the church if she could not walk properly, and he did not feel that a cane was a proper accessory to a wedding dress. Therefore, he said, he would only grant her hand in marriage to the young man who could produce the $2,000 to pay a doctor in Key West for the operation that would cure her. Of course, this made César despair, for he was sure he could never procure such an enormous sum of money. Two years passed while César tried to figure out a way to find the $2,000.

In the fall of 1904, a dispute broke out between the workers and the owners of the factory. Soon it had gone too far, and the workers went on strike. At first, the owners were not concerned, for they thought the workers would come crawling back when they didn't have the money to pay their bills and feed their families. But with the leadership of César León, the workers stood firm, and as the strike went into its third week, the owners called César to a meeting.

First, they offered him some good Cuban rum, but then they got to the point. They wanted to know if César thought he could end the strike. "What do we need to give you to get the workers to come back?" they asked him. After thinking for a moment, César said he could have the workers back to work by the following Tuesday if the owners would just give him a certain sum of money. Of course, the owners were overjoyed. They gave him the sum he requested and waited to reopen their factories the following week. But Tuesday came and went without the return of the workers. Wednesday was the same. By Thursday, there was no doubt that César had betrayed the owners. They vowed to have their vengeance and sent for their enforcer, *el tirador*, "the shooter." Though he searched throughout Ybor City, *el tirador* could not find César León.

The owners were more concerned about their factories and their profits than their vengeance, so eventually they settled with the workers and gave them the pittance of an increase that had been requested. All the workers returned to their rolling tables, except for César León, who did not dare to show his face. But time went on, and César was careless one day. *El tirador* saw him coming out of a store and killed him with one shot.

César had come to be regarded as a hero to the people, so at his funeral at Oaklawn Cemetery, there was much sadness and mourning. And chief among the mourners was the lovely Carmen Prado, who no longer needed a cane and whose limp had mysteriously disappeared.

But César must have had a very strong attachment to Ybor City, for his figure has continued to be seen since the day of his death. Sometimes the apparition seems to be as real as you or me. Sometimes his figure is misty and otherworldly. He has been seen seated at the counter of the Dirty Shame Bar, which now sits on the site where he was murdered. He has been seen sipping café con leche at the sidewalk café at King Corona Cigars. There are even those who say you can see his nearly transparent figure in old pictures taken in the early years of the twentieth century. He appears most often in October, so you may see him during this year's Fantasma Fest.

There is no documentation of any of this anywhere. And there are certain holes in the story that give us a clue it is apocryphal. For example, most of the strikes were not about wages but about things like the *lectores* and the weighing of tobacco, and most of them dragged on far longer than three weeks. And it was almost never the owners who gave in. It is also very unlikely a common cigar worker would be buried at Oaklawn. He would be much more likely to have been buried in one of the burial grounds associated with whatever social club he belonged to. And $2,000 in the first decade of the twentieth century would have been a totally unheard of sum. The factory owners would never have been willing to hand over so much cash to end a strike. It is also interesting that the ethnic background of the characters is never mentioned. Are they Cuban, Italian or Spanish? It seems like the names were even selected so that any of the major groups could claim these people.

So it is probably not true. But don't let that bother you too much. Everyone enjoys a good ghost story. The spirit of the story is very much in keeping with the history of the cigar capital of the world. And it has been reported over and over that phantom figures are seen on the streets of Ybor City. We usually do not know who these figures are. A cigar worker? An organized crime figure? A victim or a perpetrator of a horrible murder? All these and more walk the streets, avenues and the hallways of the buildings.

James Tokely, the poet laureate of Tampa, once said that Ybor City was the soul of Tampa. It is like a paella, which is a traditional Spanish dish, in which all of the flavors speak at once. He also said that in Ybor City there are ghosts and stories everywhere you look, and they look forward to you coming back. Certainly he was talking about the spirits in cigar smoke.

BIBLIOGRAPHY

BOOKS

Brown, Cantor, Jr. *Tampa Before the Civil War*. Tampa, FL: University of Tampa Press, 1999.

Cool, Kim. *Ghost Stories of Tampa Bay*. Venice, FL: Historic Venice Press, 2007.

Deitch, Scott M. *The Silent Don*. Fort Lee, NJ: Barricade Books, 2007.

Guzzo, Paul. *The Dark Side of Sunshine*. Honolulu: Aignos Publishing, 2012.

Huse, Andrew T. *The Columbia Restaurant*. Gainesville: University Press of Florida, 2009.

Ingalls, Robert P., and Louis A. Pérez Jr. *Tampa Cigar Workers*. Gainesville: University Press of Florida, 2003.

Lapham, Dave. *Ghosthunting Florida*. Cincinnati, OH: Clersy Press, 2010.

Lastra, Frank Trebin. *Ybor City: The Making of a Landmark Town*. Tampa, FL: University of Tampa Press, 2006.

Moseley, Julia Winifred, and Betty Powers Crislip. *"Come to My Sunland": Letters of Julia Daniels Moseley from the Florida Frontier, 1882–1886*. Gainesville: University Press of Florida, 1998.

Pizzo, Anthony P. *Tampa Town 1824–1886: Cracker Village with a Latin Accent*. Miami, FL: Hurricane House Publishers Inc., 1968.

Rajtar, Steve. *A Guide to Historic Tampa, Florida*. Charleston, SC: The History Press, 2007.

Reyes, Wallace. *Once Upon a Time in Tampa...Rise and Fall of the Cigar Industry*. N.p.: self-published, 2013.

Roman, Miriam Jímenez, and Juan Flores. *The Afro-Latin Reader: History and Culture in the U.S.* Durham, NC: Duke University Press, 2010.

Rule, Leslie. *Ghost in the Mirror: Real Cases of Spiritual Encounters*. Kansas City, KS: Andrews McMead Publishing LLC, 2008.

Wesfall, L. Glenn. *Don Vicente Martinez de Ybor, The Man and His Empire: Development of the Clear Havana Industry in Cuba and Florida in the 19th Century*. Gainesville: University of Florida Press, 1977.

ARTICLES

Amrhein, Saundra, and Bill Duryea. "Ybor Concert Altercation Turn Deadly." *St. Petersburg Times*, June 25, 2005.

"The Best of the Best." *Cigar City Magazine*, September 7, 2003.

Bowers, Becky. "Columbia Restaurant Revived by Re-creating Cuban Sandwich." *Tampa Bay Times*, September 4, 2010.

Bowie, Melia. "That Haunted Feeling." *St. Petersburg Times*, October 31, 2002.

Grant, Ashley. "Spaghetti Warehouse Serves Murder with Your Meal." *Tampa Bay Times*, June 21, 2012.

Hobson, Will. "Ybor City Looking for Someone Else to Run Guavaween." *Tampa Bay Times*, April 18, 2104.

Jenkins, Colleen. "Man Gets 25 Years for Ybor City Death Brawl." *St. Petersburg Times*, July 24, 2006.

Kaplan, Michael. "The First Family of Tobacco." *Cigar Aficionado* (May/ June 1997).

Mitchell, Robbyn. "Ybor City Clubs Czar, Ritz Ybor to Merge." *Tampa Bay Times*, June 28, 2013.

Mormino, Gary. "Free Love and the Long-Haired Quack." *Journal of the Tampa Historical Society* 10 (1984).

Rothman, Cliff. "Tampa's Latin Quarter." *New York Times*, November 17. 2002.

Sánchez, Arsenio M. "West Tampa: A City Made to Fit an Opportunity." *Cigar City Magazine*, March 23, 2011.

Senior, Andre. "Ybor City Murders Contributed to Pot Criminalization." *Tampa Bay 10 News*, Mach 1, 2014.

Tampa Daily Times. "Dream Slayer Talks in Cell." October 18, 1933.

Tampa Morning Tribune. "Quiet Again Reigns: Protest of Italians Brings Investigation." September 22, 1910.

Tokley, James, editorial. "Save Tampa's Cigar Factories." *St. Petersburg Times,* December 8, 2005.

WEBSITES

blakeemory.com
cigarsoftampa.com
813area.com
historyofcuba.com
Olivatobacco.com
theritzybor.com

FILMS, VIDEO AND AUDIO

Enigmatic Anomolies. Sarantella Cigar Factory mini-documentary. December 12, 2012.

The Ghosts of Ybor, Charlie Wall: The Documentary. A Guzzo Brothers Film, September 29, 2010.

Saul-Sens, Linda, and Marilyn Mars. Ybor City Ghost Walk audio tour, November 2009.

Ybor City Visitor Center Film

OTHER SOURCES

Historic American Buildings Survey. National Park Service, Department of the Interior, Washington, D.C., 1973.

OMBV No. 1024-0018. Ybor City Application for designation as historic district. received August 1986.

ABOUT THE AUTHOR

D eborah Frethem has always been fascinated by history and mystery. She found a way to combine these two things by researching, writing and telling ghost stories, especially those that illuminate the history of an area. Although originally from Minnesota, she moved to Florida ten years ago and began to learn about Tampa Bay, which has become her new love. She previously published *Ghost Stories of St. Petersburg, Clearwater and Pinellas County* with The History Press in 2007 and *Haunted Tampa: Spirits of the Bay*, also with The History Press, in 2013. As a storyteller, she enjoys using words, both written and spoken, to paint pictures of the past. Deborah is always on the look out for new ghost stories or historical oddities, and she would love you to contact her with any such tales at deborah.frethem@gmail.com. And please visit Deborah Frethem, historian and author, on Facebook.